Lincolnshire - Contents

INTRODUCTION TO THE AREA	2	FAM...	49
THE COUNTY OF LINCOLNSHIRE	...	... G THE PILGRIM	52
THE WOLDS AND TENNYSON COUNT...			53
THE COAST AND THE HUMBER EST...			
SOUTH HOLLAND AND THE FENS		...LS	
BOSTON AND THE BASSETLAW DISTRICT		...AFT	56
SOUTH HUMBERSIDE INTO INLAND LINCOLNSHIRE		...LOVERS	56
NEWARK AND SHERWOOD		...	57
GEOLOGY OF THE AREA		... SECTION OF THE VIKING WAY	57
LANDFORMS TO VISIT		WALK TWO - SNIPE DALES	60
FARMING IN LINCOLNSHIRE	16	WALK THREE - THE PETER SCOTT WALK	61
THE RICHES OF NATURE	17	WALK FOUR - THE RIVER SLEA TRAIL	64
ATTRACTIONS FOR ANIMAL LOVERS	19	RIVER CRUISE IN NEWARK	64
JUNGLE WORLD	19	SELECTED MUSEUMS TO VISIT	65
NATURELAND	21	STEAM BREWERY MUSEUM	67
EARLY SETTLERS AND THE ROMANS	22	NATIONAL FISHING HERITAGE CENTRE	67
FROM THE ROMANS TO THE CIVIL WAR	23	MUSEUMS IN THE CITY OF LINCOLN	69
FROM THE GEORGIAN PERIOD TO THE PRESENT DAY	25	SELECTED HISTORIC BUILDINGS	71
		BELVOIR CASTLE	73
THE HISTORIC CITY OF LINCOLN	26	CRAFTS OF THE AREA	75
LINCOLN CATHEDRAL	27	BAYTREE NURSERIES	81
THE R A F IN LINCOLNSHIRE	29	BRANDY WHARF CIDER CENTRE	81
LINCOLNSHIRE AVIATION HERITAGE CENTRE	31	THE PEAROOM CRAFT CENTRE	83
		STAMFORD ANTIQUES CENTRE	83
NEWARK AIR MUSEUM	31	GROSVENOR MANOR	85
N. KESTEVEN'S AVIATION HERITAGE	33	BROADWAY CENTRE	85
TRADITIONS & ENTERTAINMENT	36	HEMSWELL ANTIQUES	87
LEISURE ACTIVITIES	37	TICS & USEFUL INFORMATION	88
SELECTED LEISURE ACTIVITIES	41	HISTORIC HOUSES, CASTLES & GARDENS	89
STAMFORD SHAKESPEARE COMPANY	41		
LOCK AND CASTLE LINE RIVER TRIPS	45	MUSEUMS AND NATURE RESERVES	91
ELSHAM HALL COUNTRY PARK	45	TOWNS AND VILLAGES	93
WINDMILLS IN LINCOLNSHIRE	48	ADVERTISERS' INDEX	96

Photographs: (GBC) Grimsby Borough Council, (LAHC) Lincolnshire Aviation Heritage Centre, (LCC) Lincolnshire County Council, ((NAM) Newark Air Museum, (FH) Fulbeck Hall, (BC/ELP) Belvoir Castle /English Life Publications, (SHDC) South Holland District Council, (G&DCT) Grimsthorpe & Drummond Castle Trust, (BBC) Boston Borough Council, (NG) Newgate Gallery, (RC) Rutland Cottage Music & Fairground Museum, (AG) The Animal Gardens, (JW) Jungle World, (NSS) Natureland Seal Sanctuary, (SSC) Stamford Shakespeare Company, (SSBM) Stamford Steam Brewery Museum, (NKDC) North Kesteven District Council, (LCL) Lock & Castle Line. **Cover Photographs Top left** - (LCC) Lincolnshire Coastline; **Top right** - (LCC) Golden Cornfield; **Centre** - (FH) Fulbeck Hall; **Bottom left** - (SHDC) Willows by the peaceful waters; **Bottom Right** - (G&DCT) Grimsthorpe Castle.

Discovery Guides Limited wish to thank all those persons, organisations, official bodies and their officers, for their kind assistance in the production of this publication.

All rights reserved. No part of this publication may be reproduced, stored in a retrieval system or transmitted in any form or by any means, without prior written permission of the Copyright Owner.

WRITTEN BY: SARAH KING
ADDITIONAL WORK BY: CAROLINE HILLERY
SERIES DESIGNER AND EDITOR:
MALCOLM PARKER
PRINTED IN ENGLAND
PUBLISHED BY:
DISCOVERY GUIDES LIMITED
1 MARKET PLACE
MIDDLETON IN TEESDALE
COUNTY DURHAM DL12 0QG
TEL: (0833) 40638

The authors and publishers of this guide do not accept any responsibility for the accuracy of the general information, tours and routes suggested for travellers by road or on foot and no guarantee is given that the routes and tours suggested are still available when this guide is read. Readers should take all elementary precautions such as checking road and weather conditions before embarking on recommended routes and tours. Any persons using the information in this guide do so entirely at their own discretion.

ISBN 0-86309-089-3
© DISCOVERY GUIDES LTD

Introduction to the Area

Perhaps the most commonly held idea of Lincolnshire is of fens and tulips - and possibly sausages! The one time **County of Lincolnshire** (now Lincolnshire and South Humberside) is a vast area of interest: chequerboard fenland with fantastic skyscapes; rolling peaceful countryside in the Lincolnshire Wolds; leafy lanes twisting their way from one picturesque village to another; miles of golden sand on the coast, combined with the fun and thrills of Skegness and Cleethorpes, or peace, solitude and a wealth of wildlife at Gedney Drove End and Gibraltar Point. It is a place to drift through gently, relaxing and enjoying the space it has to offer. It has an atmosphere of former decades. Off the main arterial routes, driving is like it must have been in the 50s, yet overall communications by road and rail are good.

Lincoln City at the heart of the region is a city of enormous and varied interest, as you will discover from this book, beckoning you from afar with the huge towers of its magnificent Cathedral perched on top of the hill. It is said that on a clear day the cathedral is visible from as far away as 30 miles (50 kms)! But you will need good strong legs to 'do' all of Lincoln, for whether you start 'uphill' at the 900 year old Cathedral and the Castle built by William the Conqueror in 1068, or 'downhill' at the Roman Arch and the shops, you will have to tackle the very aptly named Steep Hill!

The region is more or less bounded naturally by water: the North Sea and the Wash on the eastern side, the River Trent on the western, while the Humber estuary is the limit in the north and the rivers Welland and Nene in the south. Lincoln stands on what is called 'Lincoln Cliff', and to the west the land falls away with a sharp drop onto the flat plains of the river Trent, while in a north westerly direction the flat marshy 'Isle of Axholme' stretches to the river Ouse. From Lincoln to the north and east, you make a more gentle descent into the lowland farmland, through which flow the rivers Ancholme and Witham.

Beyond this agricultural swathe rises one of our country's areas of outstanding beauty. **The Lincolnshire Wolds,** as these chalk hills are known, provide an area of great charm and curiosity. Driving along the A16, one gets a good feel of the Wolds, combined with the superb views to the east across to the sea. Coming down off the Wolds towards the sea, you cross the **Lincoln Marsh**, a narrow strip of land much of which has, at one time or another, been reclaimed from saltmarsh. South of the Marsh to the County boundary on the River Nene lies the **Fenland,** which stretches in a westerly direction as far as the A15 where it meets the southern extension of the **Lincoln Cliff.**

Local government re-organisation in 1974 dealt Lincolnshire a hefty blow, carving it into two and casting aside the northern part to form an uneasy alliance with an area north of the Humber, advertised as 'England's newest county'. Even today, 16 years later, pleas are still made to reinstate the old boundaries, but perhaps the most that can be anticipated is the re-establishment of the old names of East Yorkshire and Lincolnshire as they once were.

The newly formed **County of Humberside** has been well promoted by its administration and this makes further change undesirable from the official point of view. However inhabitants of the 'cast-off' section of Lincolnshire no doubt still consider themselves very much men and women of Lincolnshire, just as their counterparts on the opposite bank consider themselves Yorkshiremen and women. When travelling around **South Humberside**, as it is known, you get little sense of it being anything other than Lincolnshire. There seems to be no obvious and natural boundary.

While Lincolnshire seems at first sight to be a county full of villages and farmland, on closer inspection it can be seen that it also has some handsome towns of very great historic interest, notably Stamford and Boston. In the past, many influential and noble families have made their homes here, so that there is a wealth of **stately homes and historic buildings** to visit: Burghley House, Stamford; Gainsborough Old Hall; Gunby Hall, Spilsby; and Tattershall Castle, near Woodhall Spa, to name but a few. While making your way round the area by car, bicycle or on foot (the latter two being most acceptable and enjoyable ways of doing so!) you will come across **museums of all varieties,** many associated with historical places and buildings such as Baysgarth Museum, Barton-upon-Humber, but also some catering for special interests such as Rutland Cottage Music Museum near Spalding, the National Cycle Museum at Lincoln, the Battle of Britain Memorial Flight at RAF Coningsby, and many windmills.

The County of Lincolnshire

The County of Lincolnshire does, as we have already observed, have a remarkable homogeneity of character in terms of its landscape. Only the Wolds - and they are modest in height - interrupt the spreading miles of farmland which stretch all the way to the sea. And yet within this County is all the variety one could possibly wish for, in terms of attractions to visit and things to do.

First of all, it is eminently a County in which you can immerse yourself in the traditional, English country way of life. People in Lincolnshire have never been anything other than farmers. The emphasis of farming may have shifted, from crops to sheep and back again, but agriculture of one sort or another is an uninterrupted tradition here and the landscape it has produced is, as a result, remarkably unspoilt by industry or ugliness of any kind.

The presence of the RAF has admittedly altered some of the inland areas of the County, but the airfields, and the attractions now based on and around them, have their own particular fascination to offer the visitor. (A special feature in this book looks at the RAF in Lincolnshire).

Lincolnshire takes especial pride in its Museums, and there is no better starting point for understanding something of the history of this fascinating County. Where, for instance, can you see five Spitfires, two Hurricanes and a Lancaster? Where can you be locked in a 'vertical coffin' in a prison chapel and where can you still see working four-sailed, five-sailed, six-sailed and eight-sailed windmills? Do you know which world famous scientist was born in Lincolnshire? Or where the first ever military tank was designed and built? The answer to these and many other questions can be found in the County's Museums and tourist attractions.

The Museums and other attractions run by Lincolnshire County Council contain a wealth of fascinating objects and information covering all aspects of life from the prehistoric period to the present day and are all well worth a visit. Please note that those Museums in Lincoln itself are detailed in the chapter on 'The City of Lincoln.' Here, therefore, we look briefly at some of the County's other remarkable museums.

Stamford is widely acknowledged to be one of the finest small towns in England and a visit to **The Stamford Museum** is a 'must' for anyone who wishes to appreciate fully the town and its wonderful buildings, from its importance as a medieval burgh, through its Georgian heyday, to industrial prosperity in the Victorian period. Visitors can also find out about the local custom of bull-running and see a set of clothes worn by Daniel Lambert, the famous 'fat man' who died in Stamford in 1809 weighing 52 stone, 11 pounds.

Sir Isaac Newton, the world famous scientist referred to above, was born at Woolsthorpe, a few miles south of Grantham. He went to school in Grantham and the **Grantham Museum** now contains information and objects relating to this brilliant man, including a reconstruction of one of his experiments. **Margaret Thatcher**, so prominent in the life of this country in recent years, is also represented in her home town museum, with photographs, memorabilia and a unique selection from her wardrobe. The Museum also has displays charting the history of the town through the ages.

The Museum of Lincolnshire Life (see 'The City of Lincoln') has a sister museum at Skegness - the **Church Farm Museum**. This is the county's only open-air museum and shows life on a typical small farm at the turn of the century. The farmhouse is fully furnished to that period and the farm buildings house much equipment that would have been in use at that time. In addition, visitors can explore the 'mud & stud' cottage, which was moved to the site a few years ago, and enjoy a cup of tea in the barn cafe. Both these museums have temporary exhibitions and regular events, craft demonstrations and other activities.

Finally, at Coningsby, between Sleaford and Spilsby, the RAF's **Battle of Britain Memorial Flight** is open to the public. Paying tribute to those members of the Royal Air Force who gave their lives in the Second World War, this unrivalled collection of aircraft and associated memorabilia provides a unique insight into those troubled times. For further details of this attraction, please see the chapter on **'The RAF in Lincolnshire'**.

When you visit Lincolnshire make sure you discover Lincolnshire's lively Museums and attractions. And by the way, the windmills are at Lincoln, Burgh le Marsh, Alford, Boston, Sibsey and Heckington - and they are detailed in the chapter on **'Windmills in Lincolnshire'**.

The Wolds and Tennyson Country

This beautiful and peaceful farming area is a group of chalk hills forming the southern extension of the Yorkshire Wolds. From a northerly point on the Humber between Barton-upon-Humber and Barrow upon Humber, they stretch as far as 40 miles (64 kms) widening at their southern limit to 15 miles (24 kms) between Horncastle and Spilsby.

The Wolds have been weathered over the centuries to give these lovely, smooth, gently rounded hills. As they fold into one another, valleys nestle in between in which you will find a wealth of charming villages. Rain percolates rapidly through the thin layer of chalk soil on top of the Wolds, so habitation has centred in the places where the water comes to the surface. A glance at the map reveals very few rivers. The Rase, the Lud and the Bain have their origins in the Wolds before flowing off into flatter regions.

Traditionally an excellent sheep farming area, it has probably been farmed for the past 4,000 years. At Blechford near Horncastle, stone axes have been discovered belonging to Neolithic settlers. Bronze Age burial grounds have been documented and several round barrows can still be seen at Bully Hills near Tathwell. **The Bluestone Heath Road,** at Calceby, and the **High Street,** from Horncastle to Caistor, are ancient trackways used well before the Romans. In later years when the Romans encamped at those two towns, they no doubt used the trackways. The Angles and the Danes settled here and, by the time of the Domesday book, the Wolds had become a heavily populated area.

Vast numbers of sheep have been reared on the grassy slopes of the Wolds. In the Middle Ages, along with other parts of the County, the Wolds contributed greatly to the enormous wealth of Lincolnshire. Its flourishing wool trade brought especial prosperity to the small market town of Louth. But many Wolds villages became deserted in the later Middle Ages, possibly because of the Plague or movement of population to better farming areas on Lincoln Marsh.

The Wolds make **very good walking country** and this is probably on of the best ways to get the most out of them. A walk from Louth will take you to Hubbards Hills, where you can enjoy the cool shade of the towering beech trees and the glorious views over Louth and across the Marsh. **The Viking Way** is now a well-established long distance footpath, which will take the walker through some of the loveliest parts of this peaceful countryside, crossing the highest point in Lincolnshire, Nettleton, from where you can see Claxby Radar Station, the River Trent and the great cooling towers of the power stations; and as you draw nearer to the actual village of Nettleton, you will spot a huge column in the Caistor direction which is the Pelham Pillar. This curious edifice was erected in 1849, in celebration of the planting of 12 million trees by Lord Yarborough!

Fine views are a feature of the Wolds and a visit to the Red Hill Nature Reserve near Goulceby village will combine a splendid panorama with a look at one of Lincolnshire's last remaining areas of downland, along with the exposed seam of red chalk. The small Wolds market towns are most attractive and thriving, with a history spanning centuries: Caistor with its fine C19th buildings; Louth with its superb Parish Church of St. James dominating so graciously the elegant town; Horncastle with its antique shops; Alford with its craft fair; and Spilsby with its bustling market on Mondays and its connections with the C19th Arctic explorer Sir John Franklin.

But, an even greater charm and delight is to be found in the villages of the Wolds. In the south, the area known as **Tennyson Country** does indeed have that 'calm and deep peace' described by the C19th Poet Laureate. The villages of Somersby, Bag Enderby, Tealby, Tetford and Harrington, with which he was associated, could perhaps move all to poetry - or at least to the understanding of why Tennyson himself was so moved. Just stand in Bag Enderby churchyard and look at the graceful trees and the wonderful views; feel the space, listen to the larks, and you can feel that calm and peace - well worth searching for in these hectic days! But this tranquillity can be found all over the Wolds. Many villages have fascinating churches to explore, and good pubs, with a warm welcome, in which to partake of a pint of good country ale, and perhaps taste a succulent Lincolnshire sausage!

These days the large open stretches, once downland, are covered in barley interspersed with oilseed rape. When the rape is in flower the splashes of vivid yellow seem artificial, but we are learning to accept it as a normal progression in the farming year and, indeed, the brilliant colour does much to set off the contours of this marvellous countryside and make the views all the more striking.

The Coast and the Humber Estuary

The Lincolnshire Coast runs from the southerly County boundary, by the River Nene, north-westerly along the Wash to the mouth of the River Well, and then turns in a north easterly direction to Boston Deeps, round Gibralter Point, from which it makes a smooth curve to the north. At Humbertson, it becomes the **South Humberside coastline** of the Humber Estuary, turning inland due west along the Humber as far as Goole.

This coastline varies from one extreme to another. Some parts are densely populated and others are quite deserted. But these great contrasts are what give the coastline its very great interest. Places which are free from humans are usually home to a wealth of wildlife - and this was never more true than in the case of this particular seaboard! The **Wash Bank** in the south, so much beloved by the late **Sir Peter Scott**, is a haven for wildfowl and was doubtless the inspiration for many of his paintings. The tidal mudflats and saltmarshes are created by the rivers Nene, Welland and Witham, carrying silt and clay and depositing it as they flow into the Wash. This makes a home for many small creatures, which in turn make a splendidly tasty feeding ground for many waders, particularly geese and duck visiting in winter. Access can be made to waymarked paths on the raised seabanks at Gedney Drove End, Holbeach Marsh and Freiston Marsh for example. Sand-dunes have been building up at Gibralter Point for centuries and, as a result, the coastline continues to creep even further into the sea, leaving wider expanses of habitat for wildlife, both salt and fresh-water.

Rounding the point, we arrive at our first resort on the Lincolnshire coast, **Skegness**, immortalised by the Jolly Fisherman poster earlier this century. The slogan 'Skegness is so bracing' is very apt, as the North Sea rushes across the spreading golden sand, making the air so fresh you can smell it! A small port existed here in Tudor times, often ravaged, sometimes to virtual extinction, by the unrelenting sea. It was only about a century ago that it became popular as a holiday resort, chiefly thanks to the Earl of Scarborough. From here, the holiday coastline continues with the golden sands to Ingoldmells, where once the Romans extracted salt but which more recently became the home of the first ever Butlins Holiday camp. Just a little further up the coast you come to other popular seaside resorts. **Chapel St. Leonards** has a pleasant beach, donkey rides and everything for a real family holiday as does **Mablethorpe**. But after the comparatively calm days of a summer season, the North Sea can whip up in the winter and the huge tides can cause untold damage, the worst in recent times being in 1953.

Another long stretch of old dunes, marshes and mudflats spreads from Mablethorpe right the way to the mouth of the Humber Estuary, where we pass on into South Humberside at **Cleethorpes**. A bustling holiday resort with all the latest in entertainment, this town had very humble origins in the village of Old Clee, whose church has a Anglo-Saxon tower. Cleethorpes becomes Grimsby without one really noticing the distinction. **Grimsby** stands on the site of an Iron-Age village, the reconstruction of which can be seen in the town today in Weelsby Avenue. The fortunes of Grimsby have fluctuated, but the arrival of the railway in 1848 was the beginning of its rise to become the premier fishing port in the country, as displays at the **National Fishing Heritage Centre** show. Fewer trawlers leave Grimsby for the depths of the North Sea today but the industry thrives, as the bustling fish docks and frozen fish finger factories testify.

Up the coast is **Immingham**, once a little village, whose first dock was built at the turn of the century, and **Immingham Museum** has an exhibition showing the role of the railway in the area. It is now fast becoming one of Britain's greatest container ports. With 1992 in mind, and despite the Channel Tunnel, it is making a bid to become the busiest, as it sees itself (along with Hull on the north bank) as the natural gateway to Europe.

Following the estuary into the Humber at Goxhill Haven, the bank bounds fine farmland, well known to the Romans who had a crossing to the north bank at South Ferriby. Other ferries have all had their day, being superseded by the magnificent **Humber Bridge**, the longest single-span suspension bridge in the world. East of the bridge are worked-out clay pits, now flooded and used in part for sport - fishing, windsurfing and sailing - and part for a Nature Reserve. The pits were left after the extensive extraction of the excellent alluvial clays, once used to make bricks and tiles. The range of wildlife in the reedbeds and marshes is great, and both sides are furnished with hides. The importance of shipping in the Humber can be appreciated from here.

Enjoy the hospitality of the Crest Hotel

All 125 bedrooms have ensuite facilities, colour Television, Tea and Coffee making facilities

Adjacent to Freshney Place Shopping Centre and near the fish docks and excellent Fishing Heritage Centre.

It is a great base for visiting, Cleethorpes and the Lincolnshire Wolds, Midway between the historic towns of York and Lincoln

**ST. JAMES SQUARE
GRIMSBY
SOUTH HUMBERSIDE
DN31 1EP
TEL: 0472 359771   FAX: 0472 241427**

A TRUST HOUSE FORTE HOTEL

P.S. Lincoln Castle

A trip to Grimsby isn't complete without a visit to the Paddle Steamer Lincoln Castle Recently refurbished since its retirement from crossing the Humber Free admission to explore this historic vessel - including the magnificent engine room

TRY THIS UNIQUE DINING EXPERIENCE

The crew welcome you on board for Morning Coffee - Bar Lunches Carvery and A La Carte Restaurant W.M. Younger's Traditional Ales Moored alongside the Heritage Centre Alexandra Dock Grimsby Tel 0472 242945

MAKE YOUR VISIT COMPLETE WITH OUR DISCOVERY SERIES OF PUBLICATIONS

TITLES INCLUDE:

Lake District, North York Moors & Coast, Historic City of York, Yorkshire Dales, City & County of Durham, Peak District, Hadrian's Wall, Northumberland Coast, Teesdale and the High Pennines, Scottish Borders, Dumfries & Galloway, Cotswolds, London, Northumberland National Park, Lincolnshire, South Pennines and Lancashire

WIDELY AVAILABLE THROUGHOUT THE COUNTRY OR BY MAIL ORDER FROM:

Discovery Guides Ltd.
1 Market Place, Middleton-in-Teesdale, Co Durham DL12 0QG.
Telephone 0833 40638

THE BEST OF BRITAIN

Spend a Day in a Different World

SKEGNESS

NO OTHER HOLIDAY COMPANY OFFERS SUCH A WIDE RANGE OF VALUE PACKED MODERN ENTERTAINMENT AND SPORTS FACILITIES ALL INCLUDED IN THE ADMISSION PRICE.
* SUB-TROPICAL WATERWORLD - "FUNSPLASH"
* FUNFAIR RIDES
* INDOOR SWIMMING POOL "THE BEACH CLUB"
* OUTDOOR FUNPOOL (WEATHER PERMITTING)
* FEATURE FILMS
* ADVENTURE PLAYGROUND
* CHILDRENS THEATRE
* DARTS & SNOOKER
* BOATING LAKE
* MONORAIL RIDES
* ROLLLERSKATING
* TENNIS & TABLE TENNIS

Open: 10.00am to 6.00pm every day from 27th April to 25th October (Excluding 21st -27th of September)

ADMISSION FROM £3 PER PERSON.
DISCOUNTS FOR PARTIES.
FAMILY TICKETS AVAILABLE
TEL: (0754) 2311

Butlin's
HOLIDAY WORLDS AND HOTELS

Smiths FANTASY WORLD Cleethorpes

• ADVENTURE PLAYGROUND
• TODDLERS SOFT PLAY AREA
• WITCHES CAVE
• CAFETERIA - HOT MEALS AVAILABLE   
• SUPERVISORS AVAILABLE
• LICENSED BAR IN COMPLEX
• BABY CHANGING AREA
• NEW ATTRACTIONS FOR 91

A MUST FOR CHILDREN'S PARTIES RAIN OR SHINE -
THE WEATHER ALWAYS FINE AT - FANTASY WORLD

SOUTH HOLLAND Lincolnshire
'The Heart of the Fens'

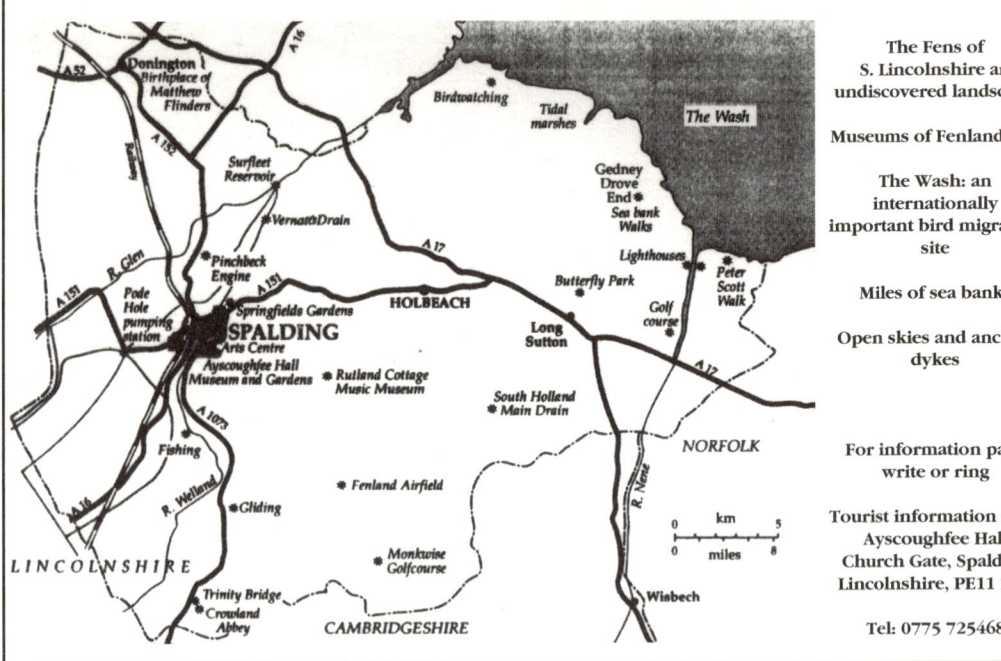

The Fens of S. Lincolnshire an undiscovered landscape

Museums of Fenland Life

The Wash: an internationally important bird migration site

Miles of sea banks

Open skies and ancient dykes

For information pack write or ring

Tourist information (DG)
Ayscoughfee Hall
Church Gate, Spalding
Lincolnshire, PE11 2RA

Tel: 0775 725468

Ayscoughfee Hall
The Museum of South Holland and the Lincolnshire Fens
Churchgate, Spalding, Open Daily except winter weekends.
Tel: (0775) 725468

Pinchbeck Engine
and Land Drainage Museum
Steam beam engine driving a scoop wheel erected 1833 now restored to working order.
West Marsh Road, Pinchbeck
Open Daily April-October.
Tel: (0775) 725468

South Holland and the Fens

South Holland in the Lincolnshire Fens, one of the undiscovered and most unspoilt landscapes in Britain, has, during the last 2,000 years, been drained and embanked by a succession of landowners and engineers; the resulting farmland is amongst the most fertile in Britain. The tranquil countryside, with its vast skies, borders on **The Wash,** which enables birdwatchers and wildfowlers to enjoy the solitude of the huge marshes which stretch for miles around the coast; they include two **Nature Reserves,** both managed by the RSPB. Coastal walks have been created, including one in Sutton Bridge, where naturalist **Peter Scott** lived in the 1930s and where he developed his lifelong interest in wildfowl.

Lincolnshire is famous for its **fine churches** - and South Holland's are amongst the most impressive. They testify to the wealth generated by wool and cattle during the Middle Ages. In more recent centuries, corn and horticultural crops have been grown and each spring thousands of hectares of daffodils make a dazzling display. Very few tulips are now grown in the fields but there are still sufficient for the spectacular, internationally famous **Spalding Flower Parade,** which takes place on the first Saturday in May, with festivities and entertainments also taking place on the following two days. The **South Holland Church Flower Festival,** is held from the end of April into the second week in May, around the time of the Spalding Flower Parade. Concurrent with the Flower Festival is the month long **South Holland Arts Festival,** which starts during mid-April. Arts information and bookings: Contact (0775) 725031.

Visitors can see a wonderful display of spring flowers in the show ground at **Springfields,** outside Spalding, which is one of Britain's premier show gardens; its expertise in providing first class flower displays being world-renowned. South Holland is also noted for its exceptional **garden centres,** which attract thousands of visitors every year. Visitors from the north can call at Birchgrove on the A16 at Pinchbeck or, if they are coming from the east, Baytree Nurseries are at Weston on the A151. The newest garden centre is Rainsbury's and this is situated at Cowbit on the A1073. All these attractions have restaurants and shops selling souvenirs and quality specialist items. Coach parties are welcomed. Further details: Contact the TIC on tel: (0775) 725468.

The Butterfly Park at Long Sutton is one of the largest tropical butterfly houses in the British Isles, where you can see some of the most colourful butterflies flying freely around you. You can step into a wealth of tropical, mediterranean and temperate flowers and foliage, set around ponds, pools, streams and waterfalls.

The Rutland Cottage Music Museum, at Whaplode St Catherine, is a fascinating working museum of entertainment, from fairground to mechanical music such as pianolas and gramophones.

In Spalding is the **South Holland Arts Centre,** which houses an Art Gallery with changing exhibitions of fine art, print making and photography, a recent example being an exhibition of Manet etchings. The Centre also runs a programme of theatre, concerts and cinema throughout the year.

Ayscoughfee Hall was built by a wealthy wool merchant Richard Alwyn in the 1430s. The Hall, which has recently been renovated, houses **The Museum of South Holland,** set in beautiful gardens with famous yew walks. Its galleries tell how the area was reclaimed to become one of the most fertile in Britain. The latest gallery illustrates the history of families who have lived in Ayscoughfee Hall during the last five hundred and fifty years. Visitors can also see the C18th library which is panelled in mahogany. A temporary exhibition gallery displays local artists' work as well as an unusual addition for a local history museum: the remarkable collection of cased birds which are on loan from the Spalding Gentleman's Society, the oldest private museum in Britain.

The Pinchbeck Engine and Land Drainage Museum was established in 1988 through a unique partnership between South Holland District Council and the Welland and Deeping Internal Drainage Board. The steam engine, which drove a scoop wheel, was built in 1833, because the local drainage had not improved as expected following the 1801 Enclosure Act. During the C19th, many of these pumping stations were at work in the Fens; when the Pinchbeck Engine ceased operating in 1952 it was the last of its type. Alongside the restored engine a land drainage museum has been established and visitors can actually see the engine working. It is open daily from Easter to November and does much to bring to life the unique history of this fenland landscape.

HISTORIC BOSTON

- MARITIME TOWN, FORMERLY ENGLAND'S PREMIER PORT
- BOSTON STUMP, ONE OF ENGLAND'S LARGEST PARISH CHURCHES
- GUILDHALL MUSEUM, WHERE THE EARLY PILGRIM FATHERS WERE IMPRISONED
- LINCOLNSHIRE'S PREMIER STREET MARKETS (EVERY WEDNESDAY & SATURDAY)
- OPEN AIR AUCTIONS (EVERY WEDNESDAY)
- TALLEST WORKING WINDMILL IN THE UK

FOR FURTHER INFORMATION, PLEASE CONTACT:-
BOSTON TOURIST INFORMATION CENTRE BLACKFRIARS ARTS CENTRE, SPAIN LANE, BOSTON, LINCS PE21 6HP. TEL: (0205) 356656

The Pilgrim Fathers' Story

BASSETLAW

ADMISSION FREE

Visit this highly acclaimed exhibition, then take the Mayflower Trail through Pilgrim Fathers Country

Tel (0909) 501148

Worksop Museum,
Public Library,
Memorial Avenue,
Worksop.

Pilgrim Fathers Country — Bassetlaw

Mon, Tues, Wed, Fri 9.30 am - 6 pm; Sat 9.30 am - 1 pm

Boston and the Bassetlaw District

The ancient market town of **Boston** stands on the banks of the **River Witham** in one of the most productive agricultural areas of England. In medieval times, Boston rose in wealth and prominence to become one of the chief commercial ports in England, and remains Lincolnshire's principal port today. The town is famous for its connections with the **Pilgrim Fathers** and its namesake in Massachusetts, USA.

Dominating the town's skyline is **St. Botolph's Parish Church**, a magnificent medieval church with a majestic tower. Profits from the wool trade paid for the building of the Church (England's largest parish church), which is open 9am-4.30pm daily and for services on Sundays. The tower, known to everyone as '**Boston Stump**', is open most days, except Sundays, and may be climbed for a small fee. The view from the outside gallery (44 metres - 145 ft) should on no account be missed.

For more than five centuries, **Boston Guildhall** has served several purposes - meeting place for a medieval guild, town hall, a prison where the Pilgrim Fathers were briefly held, and now an impressive Museum. In 1607, a group of Puritans led by William Brewster and William Bradford, having been betrayed by a ship's captain, were imprisoned in the cells of the Guildhall. They were hoping to sail for Holland and religious freedom; however they were confined for a month in Boston before going on trial in the courtroom above the cells. In the Puritan town of Boston, there was much public sympathy for these people and they were eventually set free. A year later they were successful in reaching Holland, where they established their colony. Today they are better known as the Pilgrim Fathers.

Even today, the town retains much of its picturesque charm. Its many fine buildings include **Fydell House** (one of the finest Georgian town houses in England) and the **Maud Foster Mill** (the tallest windmill in the UK). The town is at its busiest on Wednesdays and Saturdays, when a traditional open-air street market is held, drawing shoppers from throughout the East Midlands. Added appeal is provided by auctioneers, pitchers and demonstrators who set up on 'The Green' every Wednesday. Here almost anything can come under the hammer - ranging from second-hand cycles and garden machinery to plants and furniture - to the delight of bargain hunters.

The District of Bassetlaw takes its name from the ancient 'wapentake', the largest medieval division of Nottinghamshire and the northernmost, lying west of the Trent and its neighbour Lincolnshire. You may be surprised to learn that the Bassetlaw villages of **Babworth** and **Scrooby** are familiar names to many Americans, for this quiet and gently beautiful area was the home of the Pilgrim Fathers, whose courage and perseverance, exemplified by their epic voyage in the Mayflower, is traditionally commemorated by Americans in their annual Thanksgiving celebrations.

For the full story, start in the market town of **Worksop**. Here, in the **Museum**, the lifelike figure of Pilgrim Fathers' leader William Brewster, a gift from America, keeps a benevolent eye on the highly praised **Pilgrim Fathers' Story** exhibition. A visit to the exhibition makes an ideal introduction to Pilgrim Fathers Country.

Then take the **Mayflower Trail** and visit the Pilgrim churches and villages themselves. The trail leaflet is available in all the churches as well as from TICs. **Babworth Church**, 700 years old in 1990, lies in a delightful glade. Here, the unorthodox worship of Richard Clyfton was to inspire men such as William Brewster of Scrooby and William Bradford of Austerfield to break away from the established church. Bradford later became Governor of Plymouth, New England, a position he held for over 35 years. In the tiny Norman church in Austerfield, the font at which he was baptised is still in use.

Brewster's Manor House, a meeting place for the dissident 'Separatist' congregation following Clyfton's removal from Babworth, is to be found near the church in Scrooby. The Scrooby Trail leaflet, available in the village and from TICs, is an invaluable guide to all the historic buildings in the village. In its heyday the Manor would have looked much like Gainsborough Old Hall, another Pilgrim meeting place, detailed elsewhere in this guide.

Allow at least half a day to follow the Mayflower Trail - and a whole day to make the most of Scrooby and the Old Hall. For further details contact **Worksop TIC,** Public Library, Memorial Avenue. Telephone (0909) 501148 or **Retford TIC**, Amcott House, Grove Street. Telephone (0777) 860780.

South Humberside into Inland Lincolnshire

The Lincoln Marsh is a narrow strip of land extending from the south bank of the Humber along the coast between the Wolds and the sea until it meets the Fens at Wainfleet. This low-lying plain is covered with boulder clay and, towards the shore, with rich alluvial silts, and therefore is first-class agricultural land.

The Romans settled here on the coast, as is shown by their sea defences between Tetney Lock and The Haven and, further down the coast, from Sutton-le-Marsh to Skegness. **The Danes** followed, and many village names ending in 'thorpe' show us where they lived. Reclamation of the salt-marsh created excellent pasture for sheep and cattle, and farming on this strip was prosperous

As in the Fens, this prosperity is reflected in the **glorious churches,** which stand proud like great chess men on a board of ploughed fields. Stone was imported with which to build the churches, as none was available locally. Fine architecture, exquisite carving, tranquil settings, these wonderful churches offer so much: Tetney, Grainthorpe, South Somercotes, Saltfleetby-All-Saints, Markby, Burgh-le-Marsh and Croft are all worth recommending. Today, farming continues and it remains a prosperous area. Fine farmhouses stand often in splendid grounds surrounded by fields of oilseed rape or barley, with the latest in farm machinery in the yard.

Following the River Trent in a southerly direction, it is easy to appreciate the importance that the river has played through the ages, providing, as it does, good navigable water to Gainsborough and beyond to Newark. Much dredging continues today, as always, to facilitate movement of river traffic such as coal transported from Nottinghamshire and the many leisure craft which now enjoy it.

A tidal wave travels up the river at the time of the March and September equinoxes. It is known as the **'Aegir'** and was given its name by Scandinavian settlers whose river god was called 'Oegir'. It is mentioned by George Eliot in 'The Mill on the Floss', and a good place to watch this impressive tidal bore is at Morton just north of Gainsborough.

South of Gainsborough, you can travel through villages where the Romans once lived and worked, such as Lea, Knaith and Torksey, where they made pottery which was transported for sale via the river Trent. At Marton village, you can walk down to the river and follow a bankside walk enjoying the peacefulness, do a bit of fishing and bird-watching and ponder on the Roman soldiers crossing the river at the same spot all those centuries ago, possibly on their journeys between Lincoln and York. Some of the villages along the banks of the River Trent are most attractive, with some magnificent houses set in the midst of prosperous farmland.

Leaving Marton village in an easterly direction, you go up a steep escarpment onto **the Lincoln Cliff.** This escarpment, along much of its length, affords extensive and interesting views across the banks of the Trent. Just off the Roman Till Bridge Road, travelling towards Lincoln, you will spot, to your left across the fields (possibly with Limousin cattle grazing), what you may think is a cathedral in the middle of nowhere! It is in fact the glorious C11th Church of St. Mary at Stow. It is absolutely breathtaking in its size, shape and detail, and if you only 'do' one church in Lincolnshire this must surely be the one.

The River Witham cuts through the limestone Cliff at a point where we find **Lincoln** itself - and that proud city with its rich architectural and historic heritage gets its own chapter in this book.

To the south of Lincoln, the Cliff is an extensive area of farmland, peppered with delightful villages and woodland. One cannot travel the length of the Cliff without becoming aware of its importance to the RAF. At Waddington, Swinderby, and Cranwell for instance, you may see a variety of the latest aircraft in action. Dotted all over the area, there are memorials to those who gave their lives in the Second World War.

This tranquil part of England is a perfect setting for many interesting historic houses: the Elizabethan mansion house, Doddington Hall, just west of Lincoln; Fulbeck Hall, Marston Hall and Belton House, all three not far off the A607; Red Hall at Bourne; and at Stamford the magnificent Burghley House.

Finally, it goes without saying that **Stamford** is certainly worth a visit. This remarkably beautiful town is fortunate to have been spared the ravages of modern development and the Georgian part of the town remains almost exactly as it was built.

Newark and Sherwood

The District of **Newark and Sherwood** is one of the first that many visitors to Lincolnshire experience, lying close to the A1 and giving access to the further reaches of the County.

Newark is in Nottinghamshire, of course, and both that County and its famous **Forest of Sherwood** immediately recall to the memory the popular hero, **Robin Hood**. There is not space here to do more than mention in passing his legend, one of the best known in England, but what did his 'merry men' wear but 'Lincoln Green'? So Robin Hood crosses the border into Lincolnshire too. There is a Visitor Centre in Sherwood Forest now, with an exhibition on Robin Hood, while in another part of the Forest is the amazing, under-cover Center Parcs Holiday Village. There is also a **Robin Hood Way** that runs through the District, while the other major route of this sort is the **Trent Valley Way**, both delightful ways of exploring this lovely area.

Newark - or, to give it its full title, '**Newark-on-Trent**' - is a very pleasing, traditional market town, overlooked by the still imposing remains of its **Norman Castle**, where, incidentally, the little-loved King John died in 1216. Another dominant feature in the town is the elegant spire of the **Church of St Mary Magdalene**, one of the most imposing parish churches in the country. In its Treasury will be seen silver from this and other local churches.

The town has two good museums, **Newark Museum** at Appletongate, which tells the story of Newark over the centuries, and the **Millgate Folk Museum**, which takes the story on from Victorian times to the present day. Other attractions are the **Palace Theatre**, the good pubs and hotels, and the enjoyable shopping, with a regular market and plenty of good antique shops and warehouses, boutiques and other shops.

Much of the charm of the surrounding area lies in its **pleasant villages**, set in a landscape of comfortable farmland. All sorts of unexpected places of interest are dotted around, such as **Newark Air Museum**, near the village of Winthorpe, or the **Vina Cooke Doll Museum** at Cromwell.

Meanwhile the village of Elston has connections with the Darwin family, and Rolleston was the childhood home of the Victorian illustrator of children's books, Kate Greenaway, whose charming illustrations are much loved even today. Other villages have no particular claim to fame, beyond their prettiness and the fact that a very traditional way of life still flourishes within them, centred on the local church, the village pub and such important events as the regular village cricket matches or clay pigeon shooting competitions.

In fact, if you are interested in the **age-old traditions of the British countryside**, you have come to the right place, for here are such delights as country fairs and agricultural shows, maypole dancing at Wellow and, remarkably, open field farming still surviving at Laxton (the Visitor Centre next to the Dovecote Inn explains just what that means).

Another delightful town that no visitor should miss is **Southwell**, frequently visited by the poet, Lord Byron and rich in historical connections. Its **C12th Minster** is a remarkable and little-known architectural gem, just one more of the unexpected delights to be found in this very surprising region.

The District of
Newark & Sherwood

Famous for Sherwood Forest and the legend of Robin

Hood, the area has so much more to discover.
The historic market town of Newark-on-Trent with its castle, Millgate Folk Museum, antiques and river trips.
Delightful Southwell with its magnificent Minster, beautiful buildings and lovely shops.
Plus the Air Museum at Winthorpe, The Dolls Collection at Cromwell, the unique open field farming system and visitor centre at Laxton and Edwinstowe's craft workshops. Or gently stroll through the farm and country parks.
All ideal for an enjoyable day out.

Further information from:

Tourist Information Centre	Tourist Information Centre
Beast Market Hill	Sherwood Heath
Newark	Ollerton Roundabout
Tel: (0636) 78962	Tel: (0623) 824545

The Geology of the Area

From a glance at a geological map it is clear that Lincolnshire is made up of more or less **parallel bands of deposits** running in a north-south direction. These deposits were laid down during the Triassic, Jurassic, Cretaceous and recent periods.

The oldest deposits are to be found in the western side of the county in the Trent Valley. The Keuper Series were laid down about 225 million years ago during the **Triassic Period** when an inland sea covered much of the north of the country. The series consists of marls and sandstones. The climate was extremely hot, desert conditions, causing a high rate of evaporation from the sea so causing vast accumulations of gypsum and salt for example. The water in the sea would have been replenished by very violent storms. Some of the gypsum found here in the Trent Valley has been worked. Much of these Triassic formations are overlain by Pleistocene and Recent deposits, but in the Isle of Axholme there are some hillocks of Keuper Marl. Fossil remains have been found in these deposits including footprints of amphibious and reptilian creatures.

The Triassic Period was followed by the **Jurassic Period** 195 million years ago, lasting some 55 million years. A change from the previous desert conditions occurred - the climate became warm and wet. The sea gradually encroached on the land eventually covering most of England, the high parts of the land forming islands. **The fossil record** of ammonites, belemnites, gryphaea and other shell creatures, and huge marine reptiles such as ichthyosaurus and plesiosaurus, give some idea of the richness of the marine life of the time. Shales, clays, sandstones and limestones were deposited.

The Lincoln Cliff which runs from the Humber in the north to the Grantham area in the south is made up of deposits from this period. Frodingham ironstone is found at the base of the Lower Lias Beds and this has been worked in the Scunthorpe area and used for the extraction of iron. Similarly the ironstone of the Middle Lias Beds has been worked in the south of the County. The Cliff runs along at regular height of about 60 metres (200 ft) above sea level, with a line of springs where the Oolitic Lincoln Limestone rests on the Upper Lias Beds. Above these are the Great Oolite Beds of limestone and clay. The Jurassic clays were laid down in the **Lincoln Clay Vale,** the low-lying area between Lincoln Cliff and the Wolds, extending from the Fenland right up to the Humber. These soft clays were gradually eroded away by streams and very much later overlain with glacial deposits.

Towards the end of the Jurassic Period the sea began to recede and consequently there was a break in deposition of material and erosion of the already existing deposits. Eventually the sea readvanced. This new **Cretaceous Period** sea was warm, teeming with sea creatures, as fossil evidence has revealed. It was a period when substantial layers of chalk were deposited on top of the eroded Jurassic beds, along with ironstones, limestones and clays. The chalk which constitutes what we know as the Wolds is part of an extensive deposition stretching from the coast in Dorset across the country eventually outcropping at Filey in North Yorkshire. An outcrop of **Red Chalk** can be seen at Red Hill, Goulceby, where it has been exposed by quarrying. This curiously coloured chalk is rich in all sorts of fossils including different brachiopods and belemnites.

The basic shape of Lincolnshire as we know it today was established by the end of the Cretaceous Period and subsequently altered only by erosion and development of river systems during the Tertiary period. **In the Quaternary Period,** which followed perhaps a million years ago, great ice-sheets spread south from Scotland and Northern England. One from Scandinavia even stretched across the North Sea to the east coast of England, at a time when the coastline of Lincolnshire followed the edge of the Wolds.

Significant modifications to the landscape occurred at this time. Melting icy water from the edge of the glaciers had the effect of affecting the flow of already existing rivers, because it carried with it material picked up by the glacier as it spread across the land. Furthermore, rocks or erratics of Scandinavian origin were deposited in the boulder clays and glacial gravels which were left behind after the glaciers had retreated. In addition, a lake formed in the **Vale of Trent** as a result of water being trapped by advancing glaciers. When this eventually drained out of the area it left behind a rich alluvium which makes today's fertile farmland. Similarly, the **Marsh** and the **Fens** are very much features of Post-Glacial times. The sea levels fluctuated, depositing mud and gravel when high, while marshland and peat developed when the levls were lower.

Landforms to Visit

In a county as flat as Lincolnshire, it is not easy to pick out landforms as such; it is more a question of picking out **land types** - wolds, marshes, fens, coastal sandbanks, mudflats and so on.

First of all, however, let us go to one of the few eminences from which a really good view over a large spread of beautiful countryside can be enjoyed. This is the **Wellingore Viewpoint and Picnic Site**, which is to be found east of Newark in the North Kesteven area of Lincolnshire. This site was originally laid out as domestic accommodation for RAF Wellingore, the airfield itself being at some distance. This was usual policy, the intention being to minimise casualties if the airfield itself was bombed.

From this site, now attractively landscaped, you get a really remarkable panorama over a patchwork of fields, divided by hedges and dotted with villages, beyond which are some substantial areas of woodland. You are looking out of Lincolnshire towards Nottinghamshire, admittedly, but this is still very lovely countryside, very rural, very English and very unspoilt.

In the foreground you are overlooking the **River Brant,** while beyond it is the spreading Vale of the **River Trent,** some 20 miles (over 30 kms) wide. These valleys were frequently flooded, a process which deposited layer upon layer of rich alluvial soil, producing the lush farmland we see today. One of the few higher areas was the so-called **Isle of Axholme**, today no longer an island but in the past exactly that, standing proud above the flooded area.

Lincoln itself makes use of another slightly raised area, the long escarpment of **the Lincoln Cliff,** which runs all the way from Grantham to the Humber. Although it rises only to a height of some 60 metres (200 ft) above sea level, this was enough to present something of a barrier, giving considerable importance to the few crossing points, such as Ancaster and Lincoln itself. Strung out all along this **limestone escarpment,** villages developed wherever fresh spring water was available.

If we now continue moving eastwards across the county, we have to divide the landforms into two distinct areas, the **Lincolnshire Wolds** which occupy the northern half of the county, towards the Humber and the coast, and the more southerly **Lincolnshire Fens,** stretching towards the Wash. The most northerly feature worth mentioning is the **Lincolnshire Clay Vale** through which the River Ancholme runs. The soft Upper Jurassic clays here were worn away by streams draining into the Humber, again producing a fertile plain. The area is now much built up and if you look at a map you will see both the Old and the New River Ancholme marked, the old being the original meandering river and the new the man-made, ruthlessly straight channel in which most of the water now runs.

This reminds us just how completely parts of Lincolnshire are a **man-made landscape**, the land having been reclaimed from flooding by an intricate and ingenious system of dykes and drainage ditches.

The one area where this is not the case, however, is the one we reach next, the **Lincolnshire Wolds.** This high tableland of chalk, dissected by streams and valleys, is the major landform feature of the county, a lovely area of folded and gently ridged hills, which was the **prime inspiration for Tennyson,** who wrote of the 'calm and deep peace' he experienced here.

The Wolds only reach a height of about 165 metres (550 feet), so they are hardly mountainous, but they do give some excellent views, as at Red Hill, where you can gaze over the Lincolnshire Clay Vale just described.

Travelling the other way, towards the coast, the remarkable **Lincolnshire Marshes** intervene, a 10 mile (16 km) wide band of fertile land, where the sea is only kept at bay by a system of reed-fringed drainage channels. Remember, after all, that such places as Tetney and Grainthorpe were once on the coast! Needless to say, **the riches of the birdlife here are remarkable**, and can be enjoyed at such places as Tetney Haven and the Saltfleetby and Theddlethrope Dunes.

Mention of dunes reminds us, of course, of the beautiful sandy beaches to be enjoyed a bit further south, at such resorts as **Mablethorpe and Skegness,** and inland from them lie the extraordinary fens, that low-lying, misty area, where again a system of dykes and ditches has produced a very distinctive landscape, one you could not possibly mistake for any other part of Britain.

Farming in Lincolnshire

The farmland in Lincolnshire, as has been stated several times in this guide, is some of the most productive in the country. The rich alluvial plains produce **the landscape that Tennyson described** in those very well known lines which introduce his poem, 'The Lady of Shalott':

> On either side the river lie
> Long fields of barley and of rye,
> That clothe the wold and meet the sky...

It is, in fact, the same landscape that that indefatigable traveller, **Celia Fiennes**, described some two hundred years earlier, 'A prospect... shewing the diversityes of Cultivations and produce of the Earth; the Land is very rich and fruitfull... green Meadows with fine Corn fields... and Plaines and Rivers and great Woods'. Even then, of course, it was **very much a man-made landscape**, and this is why it is important to understand a little of Lincolnshire's farming past.

The Wolds were always fertile and were farmed from the beginning as a crop growing area, even in the early Middle Ages. **Norman farming practices**, as imported by the barons and clergy who came over with the Conqueror and soon established themselves as major landowners, **led to great improvements in land management.** Their efficiency was far greater than anything the native people had previously achieved and they farmed on a far larger scale - although, it must be remembered, they also set aside large tracts of land as hunting parks.

In the late medieval period, however, the emphasis began to shift with the enormous increases in wool prices and improved communications with the Continent. **Sheep farming began to play a much more dominant role** and the Lincolnshire farmers grew wealthy, as they turned over their arable fields to sheep.

The magnificence of their homes and especially their churches bears witness to this greatly increased prosperity. Fine farm buildings were built too, being added on to existing farms as the need dictated. This explains why so many Lincolnshire farms have such extensive ranges of farm buildings. The earlier farms were usually found at the heart of villages, having grown up organically, attracting a small community of farm workers and accommodating them nearby. Arable farming was always labour intensive, of course, until the development of mechanical reapers, threshers and so on.

When the move to sheep farming came, however, outlying farms began to be built, more remote from the villages because far fewer workers were needed to run them. Indeed one man, with a couple of dogs, could manage most of the year on his own. This led to a certain amount of hardship for the former farm-hands.

When arable farming started to move back into the ascendant, however, purpose-built buildings were needed anew, such as grain stores, stables for the heavy horses who did the ploughing, and eventually buildings in which to house the new agricultural machinery. And of course, it was once again necessary to accommodate large numbers of men 'on the job', so farmworkers' cottages were added on to what had previously been little more than 'crew yards.'

At the time of the **Acts of Enclosure**, considerable battles were fought in some areas of Lincolnshire over whether fields should be enclosed or should be left to be farmed 'in common', that is, as common land. In the end, however, almost the entire landscape of Lincolnshire, with the exception of parts of the Wolds, was indeed parcelled up and marked out, divided by walls or hedges. **Many of these field divisions have subsequently been removed,** to the benefit of the farmers, no doubt, who prefer huge, uninterrupted fields that are easy to plough, sow and reap - but to the detriment of the countryside and its wildlife. Even so, **the losses of hedges and small pockets of woodland** are not nearly as bad in Lincolnshire as in parts of East Anglia, for instance.

Moreover, perhaps just in time, it has now been realised that too much removal of hedges allows serious wind erosion to occur, stripping off the fertile topsoil and debilitating the ground beneath. The result is that Lincolnshire still presents very much the traditional, English arable landscape, even though it is now sometimes punctuated by glaring fields of oilseed rape or unexpected expanses of flowers. These last, of course, have been the small farming revolution of the C20th in Lincolnshire, and no doubt other products will acquire popularity in years to come. That, after all, is what successful farming is all about.

The Riches of Nature

Lincolnshire boasts a number of **wildlife habitats which are not to be found anywhere else in Britain**, and for this reason it is an especially rewarding place for the naturalist to visit.

The Wolds have their own great beauty, these gently rolling hills now largely covered in cornfields. In the past, however, they were abandoned as arable farming areas, in favour of sheep, and this explains the presence of a number of 'lost' villages, though others were lost as a result of the Black Death in the mid C14th. Sheep nibble grass closely and this produces **a flower-rich pastureland** which is still to be found in a few areas, but most of the Wolds have now been turned back to the plough and there is no doubt that farming in vast, monocultural blocks is not helpful to wildlife.

The lapwing or plover remains happy here, however, and other **birds** include the partridge, which loves nothing better than to nest in a corn field. Smaller birds include larks and meadow pipits. On the steeper, uncultivated hillsides, the traditional flowers of the Wolds will still be found, such as rock roses, kidney vetch, a number of rare orchids and sometimes the beautiful autumn gentians - and they, in turn, attract a number of **butterflies and moths.**

Fierce easterly winds sweep the Wolds, however, and tree cover, except where it has been specially planted for shelter, is scarce, so this is not always the hospitable landscape it may seem to be in summer.

Between the Wolds and the sea, there lies **the Marshland**. This wide coastal plain, also heavily cultivated but with large areas of reeds and mud, is host to a whole range of wildlife. The winds play their part here, too, though, building up **sand dunes and saltmarshes** along the coastal fringe.

Only just into Lincolnshire, south of Grimsby, is **Tetney Haven**, a marvellous place for visitors who want to explore this marshland landscape. Being so close to Grimsby, trawlers and oil tankers are regularly seen, but Tetney Haven itself, once a hive of shipping activity, is now very quiet. It used to give access to the Louth Navigation, but the canal as such was closed in 1924 and the channel is now only used as one of the many drains. **Seabirds**, such as little terns, are seen in great numbers at Tetney Haven and the mudflats are visited by large flocks of Brent Geese every winter, while such birds as reed warblers are found in the marshland reed beds. You can visit the Reserve by appointment between April and August but do please be warned: The thick reed beds can conceal overgrown drains and ditches and you should stick to marked routes.

If we now move to the **Fens,** let us immediately counter the cry that tends to come from Cambridgeshire, that there is no true fenland in Lincolnshire. It is true that there may be nothing left in Lincolnshire to match the remarkably unspoilt Wicken Fen, but there are nevertheless areas which can hardly be called anything other than fenland and which harbour much of the wildlife typical of the fens.

Not all of this fenland is found in the south of the County, incidentally. There is fenland around the **Isle of Axholme**, which is only just to the south of the Humber Estuary. But the majority of the Lincolnshire fenland is indeed in the south, bordering on **the Wash.**

A fen, strictly speaking, is undrained peatland in which reeds and other plants grow actually in the water; and it is the presence of peat which distinguishes the true fens from the marshland already described. From the earliest times, men in this area tried to drain the fens, to make use of the rich, peaty soil beneath the water level. As well as food grains, such as wheat and oats, **the early fenland farmers** grew flax and hemp, coarse, reedy plants whose strippings could be woven into cloth.

Otters are among the creatures which delight in the fenland habitat and numerous **water-loving birds** are seen, not least the very recognisable heron. There can be no large bird which lifts off water so noiselessly and elegantly as a heron, and its delicate grey colouring seems to suit this strange, misty landscape. Indeed, as portrayed in a novel such as Graham Swift's 'Waterland' (located more in Cambridgeshire than here but portraying a very similar setting), the Fens can seem quite forbiddingly silent and lonely. They are among those landscapes that polarise responses most: The Fens are somewhere you love for their wildness or in which, quite literally, you go mad.

For a full list of sites to visit, see 'Attractions for Animal Lovers' and 'Museums and Nature Reserves'.

GO WILD ABOUT
Lincolnshire!

Hurry along and get a copy of the Lincolnshire and South Humberside Trust for Nature Conservation's
COUNTRYSIDE EVENTS LEAFLET

Over 50 events being held both on and off the Trust's Nature Reserves.
YOUR CHANCE TO EXPERIENCE WILDLIFE FIRST HAND!
Send a s.a.e to:

LINCOLNSHIRE AND SOUTH HUMBERSIDE TRUST FOR NATURE CONSERVATION

THE MANOR HOUSE ALFORD LINCOLNSHIRE LN13 9DL.
TEL.: (0507) 463468 Fax 466075

A small farm centre and nature trail for the family between Nottingham, Grantham and Leicester

Our Little Farm, Lodge Farm
Plungar, Nottingham
NG13 0JH.

Telephone: Harby (0949) 60349
Follow the brown-and-white signs reading "Small Farm Centre"

THE COMPLETE TROPICAL EXPERIENCE

* Walk-through Tropical Garden
* The biggest Insect & Spider Display in the U.K.
* Lily Pool
* Birds & Butterflies
* Reptiles
* Outdoor Conservation Garden
* Wildlife-theme Gift Shop

**JUNGLE WORLD
AND
MINI-BEASTS ZOO**
The Boating Lake, Cleethorpes,
South Humberside, DN35 0AG.
Tel: (0472) 602118, 822752, 77821

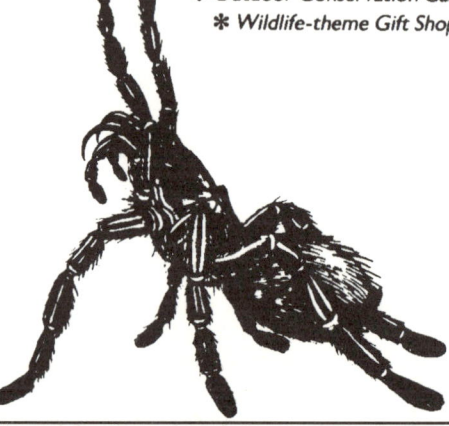

Large Coach and Car Park Snack Bar
OPEN ALL YEAR ROUND 10.00 a.m. - 5.00 p.m. Summer; 10.00a.m. - 3.30p.m. Winter
ADMISSION CHARGE: Please ring for details
Party and School rates available

Attractions for Animal Lovers

We start this chapter with some information about the body which does most to conserve the indigenous wildlife of the area. **The Lincolnshire and South Humberside Trust for Nature Conservation** is a voluntary charitable organisation devoted to the protection of our wildlife and countryside. It has over **90 Nature Reserves**, covering a wide range of habitats, including seashore, saltmarsh, wetlands, heathland, woods and meadows. These habitats are the homes for all sorts of rare and endangered as well as more familiar wildlife - the Trust looks after everything from bats and badgers to beetles and butterflies!

Membership of the Trust entitles you to visit all the Nature Reserves. However, many are of a very sensitive nature and so only about 12 are open to the public all the time. **Special events**, such as wildflower walks, open days, moth and bat evenings, are held throughout the year. Many of these provide a peek at the 'members only' reserves and, as well as providing great interest and entertainment for all the family, they show the work done by the Trust, its staff and volunteers to manage the areas for the benefit of the wildlife.

The Trust publishes various books and leaflets giving information about reserves and events. In particular, visitors may like to note the **Gibraltar Point Nature Reserve** prospectus which gives details on booking field trips or courses (there are residential and laboratory facilities) at the Reserve, and also the Trust's Countryside Events leaflet, which gives an invaluable 'What's On' list of places to visit. Meanwhile, for information about the Trust's **Snipe Dales Country Park and Nature Reserve**, and the walk that can be enjoyed through the Reserve, please see Walk Two. More information about the Trust can be obtained from: Mary Edwards, Promotions Officer, Lincolnshire and South Humberside Trust for Nature Conservation, The Manor House, Alford, Lincolnshire LN13 9DL, tel: (0507) 463468.

Our Little Farm is a combined small-farm park and nature trail at Plungar west of Grantham, designed to fascinate children, parents and grandparents equally. Its prime purpose is to give a really enjoyable indoor and outdoor experience, wet or fine. In the traditional yard you will find various friendly farmyard animals, including **rare breeds**. There are sheep and lambs, goats and kids, pigs and piglets, calves, rabbits, geese and others - especially Samson, the big Shire horse. Most can be petted and fed with special food available at the farm.

The incubator houses fertilised eggs being kept warm. There is a 'hatch' most weekends and the emerging chicks are sure to delight you. Other pens in the hatchery contain a selection of tiny chicks, pheasants and ducklings. Lots of information inside the buildings will help you understand more about the animals.

The Nature Trail covers almost 3 hectares (8 acres) including meadow, a farm pond, part of a disused railway route and a section of the Grantham Canal. Flora and fauna include many wild flowers, coots, swans, ducks, dragonflies, newts, butterflies and many more. Leaflets are available to explain the various stages of the trail and children's interpretation panels give clear information at a manageable height from the ground.

The shop sells gifts and all kinds of delicious, local country fare, from Stilton cheese to strawberry jam. Homemade snacks, salad lunches, cakes and cream teas are served in the bright and comfortable surroundings of the Old Cowshed Tearoom.

Jungle World

Situated on the lovely Cleethorpes Lakeside, Jungle World is an indoor tropical paradise, a mini-rainforest, where butterflies and exotic birds fly amongst the beautiful blooms and jungle foliage. Colourful lizards and other small animals sun themselves in special enclosures, while fish play in the lily-pool. Jungle World also has the biggest display of insects and spiders in the UK, though these are all safely behind glass!

Outdoors is the Conservation Garden where you can sit in the sun with your own picnic, or treat yourself to something nice from the Hungry Caterpillar Snack Bar. Before you leave for home, you may want to visit the Rainbow Gift Shop for souvenirs or a special present for someone. Here you will find a wide range of gifts, mainly with a wildlife theme. Meanwhile, all around Jungle World, you will find the other pleasures of Lakeside: The Pavilion pub/restaurant, the boating lake, miniature railway, paddling pool, sand pit, nature house, Fuchsia Fantasy and, of course, the beach - in fact, as they say themselves, 'It's worth being there.'

'A NOSTALGIC JOURNEY TO THE WORLD OF THE ORKING HORSE'

Meet the Heavy Horses • See the Carriage Museum & Project Room • Visit Kiddies Korner - Rare breed Farm Animals • Take a Wagon Ride •
Refreshments in the Tea Room.

OPENING HOURS

March, April, May & June: Every Sunday, Wednesday & Thursday, 12 – 4.30pm. July & August: Sunday – Friday inclusive (closed Saturday), 12–5pm. Also open Good Friday & Normal Bank Holiday Mondays. September & October: Every Sunday, Wednesday & Thursday, 12-4pm

ADULTS £2.50 SENIOR CITIZENS £2 CHILDREN £1.50

Telephone 0754 86 286

An all weather attraction

LOCATED ON THE B1195 3M. EAST OF SPILSBY

MABLETHORPE ANIMAL GARDENS

North End, Mablethorpe.
Tel: (0507) 473346

WILD ANIMAL SANCTUARY:
The Animal Gardens is a sanctuary for many injured and orphaned wild animals, baby seals, oiled seabirds, owls and kestrels to name but a few.

LINCOLNSHIRE WILDLIFE:
Special emphasis is given to local wildlife 'through the ages' and includes Arctic foxes, wildcats and Snowy Owls.

FAMILY FAVOURITES:
In addition there are the ever popular monkeys, donkeys, parrots and raccoons. In all over 70 species! Tea gardens, souvenirs, walk-thro' aviary, wishing well, free parking - the Animal Gardens is an ideal place to visit for all the family.

COME AND VISIT US SOON! Open: Every day, March to October from 10.00am Last admissions 5.00pm (or one hour before dusk if earlier)

NATURELAND

- MARINE • ZOO AND
- SEAL • SANCTUARY

North Parade, Skegness, Lincs.
Tel. (0754) 4345.

A specialised collection of animals including seals, penguins, tropical butterflies (May to September), tropical birds, aquarium, reptiles, pets corner, animal brass rubbing etc., etc. Well known for rescuing and rearing abandoned seal pups and returning them to the wild. Open every day except Xmas Day, Boxing Day and New Years Day.

THE NORTHCOTE HEAVY HORSE CENTRE is located on the B1195 3 miles (5 kms) east of Spilsby and on the edge of the Lincolnshire Wolds. All the main British breeds of heavy horse are seen here, along with native ponies of various sizes, and all take their turn to work in and around the Centre whilst also helping to earn their keep by attending various functions all over the County. Opening hours are restricted at the beginning and the end of the year, to enable essential work to be undertaken. The Centre are strong supporters of the **Rare Breeds Survival Trust**, as both the horses and the numerous rare breed farm animals indicate.

There is a **Children's Corner**, where the younger visitors can meet the equally active farm animals. Working Dalmatian Carriage Dogs are also on duty. Wagon rides are available most days.

To allow time for the 'Meet the Horses' tour, the Carriage Museum, where there are around thirty horse drawn vehicles on display, and the video/project room, visitors should allow around 2½ hours for their visit. Full refreshment facilities are available and wheelchair access is good to all parts, including the tea room and toilet.

THE ANIMAL GARDENS, at the north end of Mablethorpe, is a zoological garden and wildlife sanctuary with a special local emphasis. You can find out about some of Lincolnshire's wildlife from the past, such as wildcats, snowy owls and Arctic foxes; and many animals from present day Lincolnshire can also be seen, including grey and harbour seals, roe deer, kestrels, barn owls and many others.

Many sick and injured wild animals are brought to the Animal Gardens for care. These include seals and usually pups accidentally separated from their mothers, as well as old seabirds and owls injured in road accidents. Those animals that can not be released back to the wild are given a permanent home at the Animal Gardens. The '**Animal Gardens Seal Trust**', a registered charity, has been set up to care for injured wildlife. Recently completed, with the help of a grant from the '**Save our Seals**' campaign, is a seal and wildlife hospital and rehabilitation pool. Many other animals have their home here too including emus, lynx, llamas, donkeys, ponies, porcupines, raccoons and parrots. Finally, there is a Tea Room, a well stocked gift shop and parking is free for visitors.

Natureland

Natureland, at the northern end of Skegness seafront, has become known world-wide for its rescue and careful nursing of orphaned baby seal pups, stranded on beaches around the Wash, and has been successful in rearing and returning to their natural environment a large number of these beautiful creatures. Feeding time is a great favourite with both children and adults. The seals like to show off their talents to the visitors, and an informative talk is given on the Grey Seals, Penguins and Baby Seals, whilst they are being fed.

The Sea Life Exhibit is displayed in a 23,000 litre (5,000 gallon) tank of seawater and is home to British sharks, rays, lobsters, crabs and many other species of marine life. Large displays of tropical marine and freshwater fish and smaller displays of local marine invertebrates make the **Aquarium** a fascinating and educational experience not to be missed. As well as the seal rescue work, Natureland has dealt with, and returned to the wild whenever possible, many unusual animal 'casualties' including dolphins and whales, a 'lost' walrus and pelican, plus many oiled seabirds and injured birds of prey.

In the **Floral Palace** you can walk through a plant lovers' paradise with tropical butterflies flying freely through the luscious vegetation around you (May to October). In another section, free flight tropical birds are the main attraction, whilst cacti from around the world can be seen in the third section. **The Tropical House** is inhabited by snakes, scorpions, crocodiles and a tarantula spider plus other reptiles and insects. These are all made to feel at home by the jungle sound effects. Another children's favourite is the **Pets Corner** where the goats, calves, rabbits, ducks, geese and chickens can all be hand fed with food available at the Gift Shop.

Natureland is a favourite venue for organised party visits for schools, Guides, Scouts etc. and every effort is made to mix entertainment with education. And when you have seen all there is to be seen, you can relax in the **Refreshment Area** or browse through the beautiful seal souvenirs in the **Gift Shop**. Natureland takes pride in its commitment to the care of animals and welcomes the opportunity to share this knowledge with its many visitors.

Early Settlers and the Romans

Prehistoric man probably arrived to find a wooded island surrounded by the swamps of the rivers Trent and Witham in the north, forest in south west and fens in south east. By 2000 BC, **Neolithic man was farming on the Wolds**, as finds of flint tools and stone axes at Blandford suggest. Trackways and barrows are attributed to this period, the ancient **Jurassic Way** crossing much of England and extending from the south into Lincolnshire, in the Stamford area, and running along the Lincoln Cliff. The Drift follows the River Glen in the south west of the county, part of it forming a footpath around Swayfield and Swinstead.

Several tracks cross the Wolds, **Barton Street** taking a line along their edge from Burgh le marsh via Louth to Barton-upon-Humber and joining **High Street** which goes from Horncastle to Caistor. **Bluestone Heath Road** crosses the Wolds on the higher ground with some splendid views in parts. The long barrow discovered at Skendleby has yielded pottery from the **Beaker Folk**, and weapons have been found at Nettleham. Round barrows exist at Bully Hill off the A16 near Haugham, and at Butterhumps south east of Alford.

The **Iron Age hill-top fort at Honnington** is well documented and the largest of its kind in the county. Found near Ancaster, it is positioned on the Jurassic Way near the spot where the Romans were to set up camp centuries later. **Other settlements** were at Old Sleaford, Owmby, Horncastle, Spilsby, Ludford, Kirmington, Dragonby, South Ferriby and Old Winteringham. The remains of an Iron Age round house have been found at Brayford Pool, Lincoln. The Witham Shield, found in the river over 150 years ago, now resides in the British Museum. Iron Age man no doubt made a livelihood out of farming and trading in salt.

An Iron Age settlement known as 'Lindon' inhabited by the Coritani tribe greeted the **Romans** when they **arrived in Lincoln in 48AD**. The Ninth Legion Hispana built a military garrison in a splendid hill top position from which the army could survey the territory and where two of the great Roman roads made their intersection, **Ermine Street** from the south and the **Fosse Way** from the west. By 77AD the soldiers had left the garrison and **Lincoln** was to become a 'colonia', (the name Lincoln, being derived from 'Lindum' and 'Colonia') a self-governing community for retired soldiers. A city of great splendour was created with colonnaded streets, fine buildings, an underground drinking water supply and a sewerage system, all surrounded by huge city walls. In time the city extended downhill to include **Brayford Pool** so that the Romans could take full advantage of the water for trading purposes.

Many remains can be seen today; Newport Arch, an original gateway into the city, is the most obvious and splendid Roman remain. **The City and County Museum** in Broadgate displays both the importance and the **treasures of Roman Lincoln** to very good effect. There is a fine model of a Roman Legion marching to their garrison made of 6,000 toy soldiers, all in uniform! Replicas of tombstones and other Roman artefacts are also displayed.

Communications between Lincoln and other Roman settlements were good both by road and water. **Ancaster,** situated on Ermine Street with a direct link to Lincoln known as 'Causennae', was a camp where many treasures have been unearthed, including a mosaic pavement, coins, and pottery. Coffins said to be Roman can be found in the churchyard and there may have been chariot races held nearby. Ancaster stone was used for their buildings. In a northerly direction from Lincoln up Ermine Street you reach **the Humber** which the Romans had to cross to continue their march north to Eboracum (York). **A camp was built on each bank** at Winteringham and at Petuaria (Brough) and a ferry operated between the two.

Till Bridge Lane, as it is called today, is another Roman road connecting Ermine Street near Lincoln with the Trent. **Settlements** at Marton and on the other bank at 'Segelocum' (where you find Littleborough now) were established. This route allowed transport of goods to and from many other parts of the country, including pottery made in the kilns at Lea, Torksey and Knaith nearby. Caistor and Horncastle both had **military camps** and were again well connected by prehistoric High Street. A great feat of engineering was the cutting of the Car Dyke to facilitate **the draining of the fens**, and Fosse Dyke which joined the river at Lincoln with the river Trent to facilitate the trading in corn, which they grew on the drained land. Traces of embankments and settlements on the coast can be seen at places including Wainfleet, Wrangle and Holbeach.

From the Romans to the Civil War

The Romans had brought to Lincoln stability and civilisation. They had introduced Christianity and Lincoln's first Bishop, Adelfius, attended a Council of Bishops in France in 314 AD. Lincoln was a prosperous town, a healthy place to live in, with trading links and good communications. Instability arose after the Romans' departure in 410 AD, with the arrival from Northern Europe of Angles, Saxons and Frisians, but eventually these Germanic raiders did settle as the C5th cemeteries at Elsham and Manton testify. **The Romano-British** were quietly farming, having deserted the Roman towns, which were by now showing signs of neglect.

The Anglo-Saxons were also farmers and they settled in small groups, in villages whose names we can spot today by their endings, -'ing', -'ingham' and -'ton' (e.g. Alvingham, Manton). By using wood for their buildings, in contrast to the stone utilised by the Romans, not much is evident today, but treasures have been discovered from burial grounds which indicate their crafts, skills and artistic ability and their trading links with France, Germany, Africa, Egypt and the Mediterranean. They established their own kingdoms, and Lincoln and the surrounding area became what was known as the Kingdom of Lindsey.

The Christian Romano-British had not, it seems, attempted to convert the pagan Anglo-Saxons to their faith, so it was not until **Augustine** arrived in the country in 597 AD that this was achieved. According to Bede, the **Bishop Paulinus** visited Lincoln in 628 AD and converted the town official, Blecca, and his family. Following this, Anglo-Saxon monastic sites and churches were established throughout the region. The site of **Crowland** today is on the spot where **St. Guthlac** took up his life of contemplation as a Benedictine Monk. Barton upon-Humber and Stow are probably the finest Saxon churches in the country, and there are as many as 47 Anglo Saxon churches or their remains in Lincolnshire.

Invasions from Scandinavia were the next to disrupt the peace. Gainsborough, for instance, was fortified to stave off these raiders, who eventually established themselves in villages, breathed new life into towns which had suffered a time of decay, like Lincoln, and created others like Grimsby. It is said that, during this period of Danish raids, **Havelock**, the young son of the King of Denmark, was abandoned in a boat and rescued by an impoverished Lincolnshire fisherman named Grim, who subsequently brought up the boy. On regaining his kingdom as an adult, Havelock rewarded Grim so generously that Grim settled and established a place which took his name and became Grimsby. Many village place-names have stems showing their Viking associations, -'thorpe' and -'by'. The active trading life established in Lincoln and the region necessitated the development of a coinage. Excavations in the city, particularly on the Flaxengate site, have revealed metalwork and pottery together with articles used in spinning, all an indication of the industrious life of the time. The significance of Lincoln was reflected in the fact that it was made one of the Five Danelaw Boroughs in the Midlands.

The Normans were fortunate to find a relatively prosperous Lincolnshire, but in order to impose his rule, **William the Conqueror** found it necessary to build fortifications in strategic places such as Stamford and Lincoln. The site of the old Roman fort, with its superb vantage point, became the site of **Lincoln Castle** in 1068. Nearby, the **Cathedral** was built in 1072, reflecting Lincoln's immense ecclesiastical importance. The diocese stretched as far as the Thames. Administration of the area operated from the Castles at Lincoln and Bolingbroke. Sadly, many of the Castles (possibly 30, including Folkingham and Spalding) built by the wealthy lords have long since gone.

The population of the County grew enormously, trade was brisk, and many **Guilds** were established. The much prized scarlet Lincolnshire cloth, along with salt and lead, was taken by river from Lincoln to Boston and thence to London or to the Continent. Over fifty places, including Louth, Spalding and Barton-upon-Humber, were granted charters for fairs and markets. In the country, farming was successful - on the Wolds and the Cliff, growing wheat and barley and rearing sheep, while on the Fens, drainage increased the land available for more oats, flax and hemp, and created pasture for more cattle. Settlements grew and many fine stone churches were erected. The Church was extremely wealthy and influential with as many as 100 monastic houses.

Unrest in 1141 led to the imprisonment of King Stephen in Lincoln Castle by the Earl of Chester. A very important Jewish community was established in Lincoln at this time and the C12th house of Aaron the Jew and the Court in Steep Hill can be seen to this day. In 1157, Henry II granted a charter to the citizens of Lincoln. Later, in 1200, King John visited to pay respects to the great bishop St. Hugh, and to receive the King of Scotland. Sadly the importance of Lincoln, Stamford and Boston began to slip away at the end of the C14th. **The Black Death** took its toll as did the **Hundred Years War**. Trading links began to favour other parts of Europe, rather than Scandinavia for which Lincolnshire had been so well positioned. Once the waterways were utilised less they began to silt up and a decline set in, from which Lincolnshire was never to recover.

The medieval period left Lincolnshire in a state. The two great barons, Lord Cromwell of Tattershall and Lord Beaumont of Folkingham, were at daggers drawn and the culmination of their ill feelings resulted in the sacking of Grantham and Stamford in 1461. Both the City of Lincoln and Boston lost much of their trade and their populations began to decline seriously.

Henry VIII visited Lincoln several times but spoke very unkindly of the City. Opposition to his **Dissolution of the Monasteries** in the region started in Louth in September 1536, support being gathered in Caistor, Spilsby, Horncastle, Sleaford, Boston, Market Rasen and Lincoln itself. A cobbler known as **Nicholas Melton** (nicknamed Captain Cobbler) and a monk from Louth Abbey played an important role in instigating the **Lincolnshire Uprising**, as it was called. A march to Lincoln of some 100,000 men was arranged. They made certain requests of the king and his reply to their demands was delivered to them in the Chapter House of Lincoln Cathedral. Captain Cobbler escaped with his life, others were hanged in the market in Louth and many monks were put to death, including those from the Abbeys at Bardney, Kirkstead and Barlings (where the seeds for the revolt were probably first sown). Of the Lincolnshire abbeys, Crowland was the last to be dissolved in 1539.

On his progress with Queen Katherine to meet King James 1st of Scotland, Henry VIII made a second visit to the region and was entertained at Nocton by Thomas Wymbish and at North Carlton by John Monson. The Duke of Suffolk also played host to his monarch at **Grimsthorpe Castle** where the young Queen, Katherine Howard, is said to have been unfaithful to Henry! She was later beheaded - but Henry had already made the acquaintance of Katherine Parr, who was to become his sixth wife, while on his stay at the beautiful **Old Hall at Gainsborough**.

Early on in the C17th, certain dissatisfactions with the Church were gathering momentum and culminated later in the **Non-Conformist movement**. Puritans had their beginnings in Gainsborough, Pilgrim Fathers in Boston and, much later on, the Methodists established themselves in Epworth on the Isle of Axholme.

Government interference in religious life was not the only aspect of life that people resented. **King Charles I** saw that the whole Fenland and Axholme area would benefit from drainage, but on a large scale and organised by him. This would give him the power to specify what was grown and to use it as he saw fit. Needless to say, small landowners on the one hand welcomed the reclamation and stabilising of their land, but on the other did not wish to have all their profits creamed off by the monarch.

King Charles enlisted the help of the engineer, Vermuyden, to plan the drainage along the lines that he had so successfully achieved in his native Holland. The king also enlisted support of men known as Participants to oversee the work, to whom he subsequently granted the newly reclaimed land! At Haxey Carr on the Isle of Axholme in 1628, local fenlanders assaulted Vermuyden's men and this resulted in the death of one of the fenlanders.

At the time of the **Civil War**, Lincolnshire found itself somewhat in the middle of things, with Parliamentary strongholds to the east and south, and Royalists to the north and in the Midlands. Skirmishes consequently occurred, with local support sometimes for one side sometimes for the other. In 1644 the Earl of Manchester led a siege of Lincoln, capturing many Royalists, killing some and looting the town.

The Battle Of Winceby in 1643 is reckoned to have been Lincolnshire's most famous involvement in the Civil War, when **Oliver Cromwell** very nearly met his end! The site of the battle is still known as Slash Lane. In 1648 further damage was suffered; several churches were destroyed and the Cathedral was attacked by marauders. Indeed, the damage inflicted on the **Bishop's Palace** can still be seen today.

From the Georgian Period to the Present Day

The Georgian Period was to breathe some new life and vigour into Lincolnshire. The clearing of the once silted-up river Welland encouraged trade in Stamford, resulting in the development of a superb Georgian town, much of which we are still able to enjoy to this day. As **Defoe** wrote it was 'a very fair, well built, considerable and wealthy town'.

Similarly, by improving the **Fosse Dyke**, under the guidance of the Ellison family, Lincoln itself began to recover. The waterway renewed links between the Witham and the Trent, thus enabling the sale of Lincolnshire produce outside the County, and the import of materials such as coal from the Midlands into the County. Having acquired the lease of the waterway, the Ellison family accrued enormous wealth from the tolls and went on to establish the first bank in Lincoln in 1775. **Connections to Boston** were improved, thereby creating a large network of navigable water in the County. The building of its **Grand Sluice** helped to stimulate trade once more and Boston became the major commercial town in the County. Similarly, Lincoln's **Brayford Pool** developed industrially and was able to provide Boston with materials to export. Meanwhile, life in the City was becoming sophisticated, with the Assembly Rooms and theatre attracting people.

In order to make the best of the land and to regulate farming, the government brought in the **Enclosure Acts**. These were intended to bring into use any waste land, which had hitherto not yielded any useful crops; to regularise the use of land which had, in the past, been over-used; and to encourage rotation of crops. Most of the County was enclosed in the early period, from 1750 to 1780, but the Marshland had to wait until 1815 for this to take effect. The combination of enclosure, improved farming methods, new drainage systems, steam-driven pumping mechanisms, erection of new farm buildings and development of new farm machinery, brought about a veritable revolution in Lincolnshire farming.

Turnpike roads and the **Great North Road** increased movement around the County and encouraged the transport of goods in and out of it. This increase in trade was further encouraged by the arrival of the railway. It also allowed people to move in and out of the County in search of work. Great estates were established and Lincolnshire landowners became very wealthy, but not without encouraging progress in farming methods.

For instance, Pelham's Pillar was erected in 1849 in celebration of the planting of twelve million trees by the Earl of Yarborough. On the Brocklesby estate to this day, you can see that this forestation has continued.

By the second part of the C19th, life as a small farmer or a farm labourer had become increasingly difficult. People left the countryside for work in the factories in the towns and, as a result, Lincolnshire became very important in the development and manufacture of farm machinery.

The Midland Railway from Nottingham arrived at Lincoln in 1846 and subsequent branch lines were laid, to connect the City with the coast at Grimsby and with Sleaford and Grantham, thus establishing good links with the main supply routes to the rest of the country. Not only did the railways create new supply lines for materials such as coal and iron for use in industry they made a day trip to the seaside a possibility! So Skegness and Mablethorpe began to equip themselves for their new-found purpose in life.

Just as York had the Rowntrees and Nottingham had Lord Trent, the founder of Boots, so Lincoln had its own **entrepreneurs**, Joseph Ruston, Robert Robey, Joseph Shuttleworth and Nathaniel Clayton, whose machines were exported all over the world. In fact, Clayton and Shuttleworth joined forces and exhibited at the Great Exhibition in 1851. Moreover, some of the first aeroplanes were developed and constructed in Lincoln, and the area became the obvious **home for the RAF**, founded in 1918.

Engineering has continued to play a major role in the life of the county. Both in Lincoln itself, along with Gainsborough and Grantham, and in the north (now South Humberside), a greater diversity of industry has become established, with the docks at Immingham and Grimsby and the steelworks at Scunthorpe. **Communications have altered** too, with such developments as the motorways, the Lincoln by-pass and the Humber Bridge. But life in Lincolnshire still goes on much as it ever did: ploughing, sowing and harvesting; breeding, rearing and grazing animals. The only thing that really has changed is the mechanisation of farming, which has turned it into an industry and big business. Nevertheless, Lincolnshire remains a great swathe of countryside, with peace and tranquillity and that 'away from it all' feeling to offer the visitor.

The Historic City of Lincoln

The City of Lincoln must be one of the most spectacular in the country, yet is still largely undiscovered by many who travel north or south using only the A1 or the M1. New road networks have made the City more easily accessible without spoiling its heart and many car parks are available. Modern amenities include good shopping and sports facilities, a country park, cinemas and a theatre.

The jewel of the city - and indeed of the County - is the 900 year old **Cathedral**, the third largest in England. It sits in a commanding position at the top of the Steep Hill, in the peaceful surroundings of the Cathedral Close. When you pass through the arch of the Exchequer Gate, this stunning and massive building cannot fail to thrill the visitor. (see the next page).

Leaving the Cathedral (or Minster, as it is also called), by way of the Exchequer Gate, you will see one of Lincoln's oldest buildings, housing the Tourist Information Centre. Straight ahead is the **Castle,** which you enter by the imposing C12th Eastgate. Within the confines of the walls is a collection of buildings set in well-kept and attractive gardens and lawns. A walk round the walls which are some 3 metres (8-10 ft) thick, gives the most wonderful view of the region. What a commanding position it must have given any soldier! Boston Stump and Sherwood Forest are visible on a clear day. The prison is an austere red-brick building (built 1787 to 1791), in which you can see the curious Victorian Prison Chapel. This was designed so that offenders could go to worship and could see the chaplain, but were unable to mix with their fellow prisoners. **Cobb Hall,** a tower set in the north-eastern part of the wall, may also have been a prison in the early days of the Castle and was certainly the site of the county gallows until the last century. Today the castle is often used for historical entertainments, such as archery, jousting and other events.

Bailgate, which boasts a fine selection of shops, leads north from Castle Square towards the Roman **Newport Arch.** Other Roman features can be spotted in the area. Setts in the road mark the positions of a colonnade, and to the left, in Westgate, excavations show a Roman well. In East Bight, close by, parts of the Roman wall remain, along with evidence of the aqueduct system. On the site of St. Paul in the Bail, where many churches have stood, a Roman herb garden has recently been planted.

Westgate leads into Burton Road, where you will find the **Museum of Lincolnshire Life,** occupying the barracks built in 1856 and well worth a visit to get a real feel of Lincolnshire and its life over the centuries. Just a few minutes' walk away is **Ellis' Mill,** open at weekends, a four-sailed mill affording extensive views across the countryside. In Minster Yard close by, is the **Bishop's Palace.** Now sadly all that remains is a ruin, but it is in the hands of English Heritage, who display what there is to give you an idea of its former greatness.

Steep Hill will take you from the Castle Square to the lower part of the town around the river. It is indeed a steep hill and, in order to keep your footing, it is better to take it slowly and absorb all the intricacies of its buildings. Externally, it offers quite a history lesson, with timber-framed buildings of the C14th and C15th. Two of Lincoln's most famous buildings, also found in Steep Hill, are associated with the thriving Jewish community of the time. **Jew's House and Jew's Court** date back to about 1180 and it is possible that they occupy the site of the synagogue.

Just off to your left as you descend the hill, down Danesgate, you will see the **Usher Gallery,** which is well worth a visit. (See 'Selected Museums to Visit'). Steep Hill becomes The Strait, as you get near the bottom of the hill and this narrow old street opens out into the wide High Street, with the C15th **Stonebow Gateway** ahead of you. Above is the castellated **Guildhall,** with its fine timbered roof made of oak from Sherwood Forest. (See 'Selected Historic Buildings').

Further down High Street, you will come to the High Bridge over the River Witham. Today the fine half-timbered buildings on the bridge are shops. Nearby is **Brayford Pool,** which has a history of use dating back at least to Roman times. This area is now being sensitively developed, and new attractions include the **National Cycle Museum.** Even now, you have not by any means seen all of Lincoln's historic buildings. There are still such treasures to explore as **St. Mary's Guildhall** and two churches with Saxon foundations, **St. Mary's le Wigford** and **St Peter's at Gowts** ('gowt' means a watercourse) - and don't leave Lincoln without seeing the **City and County Museum's** most treasured possession, one of the only four copies of the **Magna Carta,** signed by King John in 1215.

Lincoln Cathedral

The sight of **Lincoln's nine hundred year old Cathedral,** sitting as it does high up on the hill above the town, must rate as one of the most spectacular in the country. No matter how you approach the City, it beckons you with its massive towers. This Cathedral was built within the walls of the old **Roman City.** There have in fact been three buildings on this site, the first one built under the instruction of William the Conqueror in 1072 and overseen by William's own appointee as Bishop, **Remigius de Fecamp.** Regrettably, Remigius did not live to see its consecration. In 1141 a great fire spread through the cathedral and it was the third Bishop, **Alexander the Magnificent**, who carried out its restoration. But in 1185 an even greater disaster struck in the form of an earthquake. All that was left standing were the West Front and some of the western towers and another massive operation of rebuilding was subsequently undertaken with only the West front being preserved.

Henry II had chosen a monk from a very strict order in south eastern France to run a small priory, of the Carthusian order, in Somerset. Following the earthquake, **Hugh of Avalon**, as he was called, was ordered to Lincoln to be its new Bishop. Though disinclined to accept the responsibility, Hugh did eventually set about the rebuilding of the Cathedral in the most painstaking way. He was an inspiration to all the craftsmen who worked with him, but sadly he died in 1200 and did not see the completion of his work which took another eighty years. Various setbacks occurred after that: The central tower fell down and was rebuilt by 1311, and when a spire was erected on it the height reached 160 metres (525ft). The spire fell off in 1549. In a painting of the Cathedral in 1742, by Joseph Baker (in the Usher Gallery), the western towers can be seen with their spires, but they were thought to be unsafe and were removed in the C19th.

The entrance to the Cathedral Close is via the lovely **Exchequer Gate**, which brings you face to face with the magnificent **West Front,** an awe-inspiring sight which can make you hold your breath! It is a very peaceful place with well-kept lawns and a crescent of very beautiful Georgian houses which revel in one of the most outstanding views ever.

The huge nave is C13th, built in the Early English style of Purbeck marble and limestone. To the left is the **Morning Chapel**, very light and airy, with an elegant pillar of Purbeck marble reaching up to the vaulted roof. A pair of binoculars is useful in helping you study the beautiful stained glass, especially the two great rose windows known as **The Dean's Eye** and **The Bishop's Eye.** Here there is also the great C14th stone screen in Decorated style, so intricately carved with curious little figures that it could have been the inspiration for Maurice Sendak's 'Wild Things'! If you look carefully you can see remnants of red and green paint which brightened up this screen centuries ago.

In the North Transept are **The Three Services Chapels**, each one impressive by its attention to detail. For instance, in the Seamen's Chapel, the wooden altar rail is carved with a rope design and at each end stands a silver dolphin, presented in 1951 by the Admiralty. Similarly, in the Airmen's Chapel the altar rail is carved with wings and stars. At the **East Transept,** there is a small exhibition of such items as stone, tools, wood, a misericord and lead from the roof, carefully presented for blind visitors. Through a nearby door, you arrive at the **Cloisters,** a serene and peaceful corner. Leading off the Cloisters to the right is the C13th **Chapter House**, the first ever to be built in the unusual polygonal shape. The coffee shop is nearby, as is the Wren Library, but the latter is still undergoing restoration and is only open by appointment.

Alongside the unusual **St. Gilbert of Sempringham** memorial is **St. Hugh's Head Shrine**, a beautiful work of art once adorned with jewels, now ornamented with a stunning bronze structure erected to commemorate the 800th anniversary of St. Hugh's installment in Lincoln. If you stand back a little from St. Hugh's Shrine and cast your eyes up the pillar on your left, you will see the **Lincoln Imp** watching you! Turning back and going straight ahead you come to the spiritual centre of the Cathedral, where you will find **St. Hugh's Choir** on your left, with its glorious carved oak stalls and the curious misericords under the seats, while to your right is the **Sanctuary.** On its north side is the beautiful **Easter Sepulchre** and the tomb of Remigius, while on the south side is the charming **Katherine Swynford Chantry**, where Katherine was married to John of Gaunt in 1396. You complete your tour at the back of the nave, after which you may wish to visit the shop on your left, to purchase some memento of the truly magnificent building which you have just visited.

BAINLAND COUNTRY PARK

LUXURY SOUTH FACING SELF CATERING HOLIDAY BUNGALOWS

Many new for 1991 with microwave, jacuzzi and central heating for that little extra comfort. Holidays available from short breaks of 2 nights up to 2 weeks.

LEISURE COMPLEX

Free to bungalow residents. Range from 18 hole golf course par 3 to international standard tennis courts with professional coaches. Indoor heated swimming pool, jacuzzi, sauna and sunbeds and for the energetic amongst you an exercise room. We haven't forgotten the children. We have available a large adventure playground, giant chess, crazy golf, croquet and boules.

CARAVAN TOURING PARK

Secluded caravan touring park with free hot water in basins and showers. New for 1991 super pitches with high rated electricity, hard standing, own sewage and water to each pitch plus satellite TV.

Available on site - open all day - the Bistro & Bar for light meals or takeaway. Open evenings only – Poachers Restaurant & Bar. For prices and any further details please contact

Bainland Country Park, Horncastle Road, Woodhall Spa, Lincolnshire.
Tel: 0526 52903

AA • RAC • ROSE AWARD • BRITISH GRADED HOLIDAY PARK ✓✓✓✓

The Lodge Hotel
40 Nettlesham Road
Lincoln
Lincolnshire
LN2 1RE.
Tel: 0522 513001

Relax Village Style at
The Village Shop & Post Office
Hough on the Hill Grantham

BED & BREAKFAST FAMILY ROOMS
GROUND FLOOR ROOM AVAILABLE ON REQUEST
TEA & COFFEE MAKING FACILITIES
EN-SUITE FACILITY AVAILABLE
CARAVAN AND CAMPING FACILITIES IN THE
HEART OF OUR VILLAGE
VISIT OUR CHURCH WITH THE SAXON TOWER
Morning newspapers available
WALK THROUGH THE CHURCHYARD SEE THE VIEW
ACROSS THE VALE OF BELVOIR

Bed & Breakfast From £15.00 per person
Children welcome
Caravans...£3.00 per night
Tents with 2 persons £2.00 per night
.50p per add. person.

Telephone Mrs Meale 0400 50229

The Royal Air Force in Lincolnshire

Aviation in this region goes back as far as 1826, when a flight was attempted with a gas balloon, on the occasion of the opening of the Boston Gas Works. Others were to follow bringing with them excitement and near disaster, one gas balloon nearly hitting Sleaford windmill.

Lincoln was to become a leading aircraft manufacturing centre in the First World War with such names as Robey's, Clayton and Shuttleworth, and Ruston, Proctor and Co. leading the way. Airfields were brought into operation at various times in the War, including Bracebridge Heath, Anwick, Digby, Wellingore and Cranwell. All faced the horrors of the Zeppelin raids in 1916 and 1917, some of which visited disaster on several villages, notably Washingborough in September 1916.

In April 1918, the RAF was officially formed. Parts of Lincolnshire, such as Lincoln Cliff, were ideal for military airfields. The ground was flat, and there was plenty of it to give a good length for runways, while south-westerly prevailing winds assisted landing and take-off. Hedges were ripped out in some places, but in others groups of trees and woods provided excellent shelter for equipment. The flatness gave well defined accesses, easily seen from the air, and the ground drained well, thus avoiding waterlogged landing strips.

New airfields were opened up all over the County during the **Second World War** and by 1945 there were 49, including RAF Coleby Grange, Metheringham, Coningsby, Anwick, Cranwell, East Kirkby, Binbrook, Swinderby and Wellingore. Lincolnshire became the home of Bomber Command. From the very day on which War was declared, planes flew from there. First to go were the Handley Page Hampdens (nicknamed 'flying tadpoles') from RAF Waddington. New planes were continuously designed, developed and flown from the various airfields: Hawker Hurricanes, the Gloster E28/39 (the Whittle), Lancasters, Spitfires, Defiants - all the names which evoke memories for anyone who lived through those terrible days.

It was a tense time for servicemen and civilians alike, anticipating sudden attack, awaiting the call for action stations and, perhaps worst of all, waiting for planes to return to base. But the world of anti-aircraft guns, air raid shelters, blast pens, hangars and pillboxes has long since gone and you can appreciate the contribution made by the RAF, if you visit the Lincolnshire Aviation Heritage Centre at East Kirkby, Newark Air Museum, the Battle of Britain Memorial Flight or the numerous sites along the North Kesteven Airfield Trail. All are featured in the following pages.

Numerous memorials can be seen all over the County, such as those in Woodhall Spa commemorating 617 Squadron, the Dambusters. For instance, the Petwood Hotel in Woodhall Spa has its own memorial. Once a private house, the home of Sir Archibald and Lady Weigall, it was requisitioned by the RAF in 1953 as the Officers' Mess of 617 Squadron, the Dambusters. The Squadron Bar has a display of items associated with them. A memorial was erected in 1987 in the Royal Square in Woodhall Spa in the shape, appropriately enough, of a miniature dam. The 199 names of those members of the sqaudron who gave their lives are featured on it.

The major memorial, however, is in the Airmen's Chapel in Lincoln Cathedral. There you will find the Memorial Books with the 25,611 names of the people killed while flying from airfields in and around Lincolnshire.

Many airfields have since become disused, but some are bases for crop spraying mono-planes and microlights. Those which remain play a vital role in defence. New planes have been developed and tested, becoming faster and more sophisticated machines: B-29 Washingtons in the early 50s, Avro-Vulcans in the 60s and 70s, and now the Jet Provost.

Today there is the Elementary Flying Training School at RAF Swinderby, just off the A46 south west of Lincoln, where Chipmunks are flown. The Boeing E3 Sentry flies out of RAF Waddington due south of Lincoln on the A15, and at RAF Coningsby, just south of the A153, is a fighter station with the Tornado Operational Training Unit. The very familiar Red Arrows have their home at RAF Scampton, off the A15 north of Lincoln, as does the Central Flying School. Here you may see the Jet Provost, Bulldog, Tucano or Hawk planes in the air. Finally, on the B1429 north of Sleaford is the heart of the **RAF at Cranwell**, were you will find the RAF College, and the Flying Training School.

LINCOLNSHIRE'S MEMORIAL TO BOMBER COMMAND

Come and Sample the atmosphere of a Wartime Bomber Airfield

LINCOLNSHIRE AVIATION HERITAGE CENTRE
East Kirkby, Spilsby
Tel: (07903) 207

★ AVRO LANCASTER BOMBER NX611
★ ORIGINAL STATION CONTROL TOWER
★ ESCAPE MUSEUM
★ PHOTOGRAPH EXHIBITION
★ LINCOLNSHIRE AIRCRAFT RECOVERY GROUP
★ NAAFI SHOP & REFRESHMENTS

There is no charge for parking cars or coaches and there is ample space for both. The Heritage Centre is open Monday to Saturday (closed Sundays) from 10am–5pm last admission 4pm. There are reduced rates for Senior Citizens & children. Children under 5 years Free.

Situated on the A155 between Spilsby and Sleaford at East Kirkby.
THIS IS AN ALL WEATHER ATTRACTION

NEW
Undercover Aircraft Display Hall
- **NEW** Undercover Engine Display
- Over 35 Aircraft on Display
- Exhibition Hall - Aviation Artefacts & Memorabilia
- Large Souvenir Shop

OPEN April-October, Monday-Friday 10am-5pm, Saturdays 11am-5pm, Sundays 10am-6pm, November-March, Saturdays 11am-dusk, Sundays 10am-dusk.

ADMISSION Adults £2.00 Children & OAP's £1.00 Group rates on application. The Airfield, Winthorpe, Newark, Notts., NG24 2NY.
Tel. (0636) 707170

The Lincolnshire Aviation Heritage Centre

The **Lincolnshire Aviation Heritage Centre** is situated on the A155 between Spilsby and Sleaford at East Kirkby. East Kirkby Airfield was the home base of Squadrons 57 and 630 Lancaster bombers from 1943-45.

Among the many exhibits is a complete AVRO Lancaster bomber NX611 on permanent display in a purpose-built, insulated hangar. Also there is the original Station Control Tower on which the TV film 'Watch Tower' is based. The Tower is furnished in the 1940s style as closely as possible, (quite an experience in itself). It has its own atmosphere. **The Escape Museum** is near the Tower and is housed in its own building and quite vividly shows the ingenious ways used by airmen to escape back to this country. Also exhibited is Albert RN from the film of that name, together with the Wooden Horse. A scale model of the Colditz glider is suspended from the roof. Photographs and items give an insight into the many ways adopted to obtain freedom.

The **Lincolnshire Aircraft Recovery Group** also have a multitude of interesting items on display, from crash sites and other places, which have been meticulously cleaned, labelled and brought to a high standard of presentation. Visitors will also find of interest the original blast shelter situated to the rear of the Tower. This has been repaired, and is a good example of its type, simple in construction, but most effective. Not far from the blast shelter is a long wooden wartime building, housing many exhibits of **The Aviation Society** too numerous to name - but there is a considerable part of a Hampdon Bomber under re-construction which has its own story. There is also a wind tunnel model of an AVRO Vulcan bomber, a fine example of skill and workmanship. Also in this building are pre-war small aircraft, and an observer post too.

There is plenty of room to move around on concrete or grass to enjoy the country air. The visitor may well be ready for some refreshment by now and the NAAFI is just the place. Hot and cold drinks are available, as are hot and cold snacks. In the NAAFI shop there are further displays, photographs and memorabilia. Taped music will add to the atmosphere and, we hope, to your enjoyment as well.

Newark Air Museum

Since its formation in 1963, **Newark Air Museum's** collection of aircraft, aero engines and aviation relics has steadily grown to represent one of the largest, non-profit making, volunteer managed aviation museums in Great Britain. Based on an original 2nd World War Bomber Dispersal on Winthorpe Airfield, Newark, nearly half of the museum's 40 aircraft are now displayed under cover in a recently constructed **Aircraft Display Hall**. Visitors can wander past the diverse array of transport, training and reconnaissance aircraft, assorted helicopters and one of the finest displays of rare and in some cases unique British, American and European jet fighters and bombers in Great Britain.

Aircraft types on display include: Hastings, Varsity, Heron and Dove transport aircraft; Provost, Prentice, Vampire, T33 and Safir trainers; Sycamore, Sioux, Whirlwind and Zurowski helicopters; Vulcan, Canberra, Buccanneer and Sea Vixen bombers; Meteor, Javelin, Swift, Venom, Sea Venom, Sea Hawk and Super Sabre jet fighters. Some of the larger aircraft are frequently open to the public. For a small additional donation towards restoration funds, visitors can take the opportunity to look inside the rare military aircraft such as the Vulcan, Hastings, Shackleton and Varsity.

In addition to the aircraft, there is an impressive collection of aero engines, aircraft parts and aviation related relics. A recently opened, undercover **Engine Hall** features a display of 30 different aero engines. A separate **Exhibition Hall** houses a multitude of displays featuring uniforms, aircraft equipment, artefacts and aviation memorabilia.

The large **Souvenir Shop** stocks a large selection of medals, postcards, posters, badges, tea towels and paintings. **Newark Air Museum** is located on the Newark Showground off the A46 Newark-Lincoln road, and signposted from both the northbound and southbound A1 and the new Newark bypass. There are facilities for the disabled; special group visits can be arranged in advance; there is ample free car and coach parking and the Museum is open every day except Christmas Eve, Christmas Day and Boxing Day.

LINCOLNSHIRE'S Aviation Heritage

In a corner of rural Lincolnshire's unspoilt countryside you will find some of the best aviation heritage around. Why not pay us a visit and explore for yourself.

For further information contact Sleaford Tourist Information Centre, ref DG
The Mill, Moneys Yard,
Carre Street, Sleaford,
Lincolnshire.
Tel: (0529) 414294.

Battle of Britain Memorial Flight

RAF Coningsby, Lincoln,
LN4 4SY
Telephone: (0526) 44041.
Open: Monday to Friday 1000-1700 (last conducted tour 1530).
Closed for two weeks over the Christmas period.
Admission: £2.00, children/OAPs £1.50.

At RAF Coningsby, The Battle of Britain Memorial Flight operates five Spitfires, two Hurricanes and one of only two Lancasters still flying in the world today. This remarkable collection is a living tribute to all RAF aircrew and groundcrew who gave their lives in the Second World War.

"Briefings" Weekend Breaks

Explore Lincolnshire's aviation heritage and distinguished association with the RAF past and present on a special weekend break for aircraft enthusiasts.

"North Kesteven Airfield Trail"

The North Kesteven Airfield Trail booklet outlines the history of ten airfields, four still operational by the RAF, in this part of mid-Lincolnshire and a suggested route by which to discover them.

North Kesteven's Rich Aviation Heritage

For many, the highlight of a visit to the 'Home of the RAF' will be reliving personal memories of Service days. However, the **Battle of Britain Memorial Flight**, a unique living tribute to those who served and died in the RAF, and the wide range of things to see and places to visit in Lincolnshire are impressive. At its home base of RAF Coningsby, the Battle of Britain Memorial Flight operates five Spitfires, two Hurricanes and one of only two Lancasters still flying in the world today. This remarkable collection is a living tribute to all RAF aircrew and ground crew who gave their lives in the Second World War. The Flight's irreplaceable and virtually unique aircraft are maintained by a small group of dedicated engineers, whose efforts to overcome shortages of spare parts, and to acquire skills all but lost, enable the Flight to give up to **150 shows annually**, around the country, mainly during summer weekends.

Apart from these weekends, the Flight welcomes visitors to view the aircraft and see the **Visitor Centre** with its collection of wartime memorabilia. Experienced volunteer guides, many with first hand knowledge, show you round and will happily answer any questions you may have. Because of operational commitments, and the fact that the availability of specific aircraft cannot be guaranteed, it is recommended that you ring for latest details when planning your visit.

NORTH KESTEVEN AIRFIELD TRAIL

The aviation heritage of Lincolnshire is vast and, to commemorate its own particular associations with this distinguished past, North Kesteven District Council have pioneered a unique Aviation Trail. **The trail links ten airfields** located in this part of Mid-Lincolnshire, and the history of their origins and significance is detailed in the North Kesteven Airfield Trail booklet. The booklet is available free of charge from North Kesteven's two Tourist Information Centres in Sleaford and Heckington.

Four of the airfields - **RAF Cranwell, RAF Waddington, RAF Digby** and **RAF Swinderby** are still operational by the present day Royal Air Force. Marker boards identify the sites of the former airfields based at **Metheringham, Wellingore, Leadenham, Coleby Grange, Bracebridge** and **Anwick**. The Trail is designed for car-bound visitors and can be started anywhere. If joining the Trail at Lincoln, one of the first airfields you will come across is that of **RAF Waddington.** This airfield began life in 1916 as a busy training station for the Royal Flying corps. Today it is dominated by a new hangar complex, designed to take 8 Squadron's Boeing Sentry. You may be lucky enough to see an 'AWACS' E3 aircraft, with its distinct rotating radar dish mounted horizontally in front of the tail fin, approach or depart from the airfield. Perhaps the most famous resident, however, is the Vulcan Display Flights B2 XH558. In the village of Waddington itself is a memorial clock dedicated to the Australian members of 463 and 467 Squadron, who flew from Waddington during World War II and did not return.

At **Metheringham,** two miles further east from the village, on the B1189, the remains of RAF Metheringham can be seen. In 1943 Alderman George Flintham and his fellow farmers were given only 48 hours to remove their household belongings and livestock from the chosen site. The farm buildings were then demolished and trees uprooted and cleared. The site was ready for service by late October for the Lancasters of 106 Squadron, who arrived in November of that year. Two public roads now follow two of the runways which formed part of this airfield.

The Royal Air Force College at Cranwell is a famous landmark in RAF history. Though strangely enough, Cranwell owes its origins to the Royal Naval Air Service who established it in 1916 as a flying training station, where officers and cadets could be trained to fly aeroplanes, observer kite balloons and airships. With the amalgamation of the RNAS and the Royal Flying Corps in 1918, ownership of Cranwell was passed to the Royal Air Force. In 1920 the Royal Air Force College, the first Military Air Academy in the world was opened.

Visitors are reminded that Cranwell, Waddington, Swinderby and Digby are operational facilities and clearly not open to the public. Care must be taken to observe official notices and parking restrictions on the perimeters of these airfields. At former airfield sites, the land is now privately owned and visitors are requested not to stray from the public roads.

For those who would like to follow the Airfield Trail, more detailed information about the actual route and the places of interest to visit along the way is given in 'Drive Four'.

There are many exhibits to enthrall all members of the family, whatever their age, at the popular Newark Air Museum (NAM)

Aircraft and the Royal Air Force enjoy a deep and lasting association with this region

A Lancaster bomber standing outside its hanger at the Lincolnshire Aviation Heritage Centre at East Kirkby (LAHC)

A Spitfire, Hurricane, and Lancaster of the Battle of Britain Memorial Flight in front of their hanger at Coningsby (LCC)

Aeroplanes of all sizes and all types await your inspection and enjoyment at the well-known Newark Air Museum (NAM)

This fine exterior view of Fulbeck Hall near Grantham has been enjoyed by many visitors (FH)

The interesting 'Tented Room' at Fulbeck Hall (FH)

The impressive West Front of the magnificent Belvoir Castle near Grantham (BC/ELP)

The great medieval abbey at Crowland (SHDC)

Lincolnshire's treasure chest of historic buildings possesses some priceless gems

Grimsthorpe Castle, located near Bourne, not only has a most majestic appearance, but also a tremendous setting (G&DCT)

Traditions and Entertainment

In common with other parts of rural England, **Lincolnshire is rich in traditional events** which have survived, in some cases, in an unbroken line for many generations. This is perhaps especially the case with the eastern counties, which were for so many years a little 'out on a limb' in terms of north-south communications, and old fashioned ways of doing things perhaps persisted longer here than elsewhere.

Now, in the rush and bustle of the C20th, it is especially refreshing to find these old events still taking place in the age-old way. But there are very numerous newer events too and The East Midlands Tourist Board publishes a most useful list of **'Events in the Middle Shires of England'**. You will find the Tourist Office at Exchequer gate, Lincoln, tel: (0522) 531521. Local TICs will also have useful lists of events in their own regions.

Mayday celebrations are to be found at such places as Gainsborough and Hemswell, for instance. In the latter village, children dance around a maypole in the traditional manner, weaving and unweaving coloured ribbons in intricate patterns.

Agricultural shows are always a great source of enjoyment and these take place from the end of May onwards, one of the first being at Woodhall Spa. The Lincolnshire Show itself is held in June, preceded by the Lincoln Carnival a week or two earlier.

The other Carnivals, at towns on the coast such as Skegness and Mablethorpe, wait until later in the year, taking place in August. Both towns have annual **Summer Illuminations** and these same two seaside towns are also, incidentally, popular venues for **bowls competitions** - no surprise to find that this sport is so popular in a county which is so flat! Other towns which see regular bowls competitions are Woodhall Spa and Louth.

Other sporting events include regular **National Hunt racing** throughout the season at Market Rasen, the **Lincolnshire Spring Horse Trials** in April, **Autumn Horse Trials** in October, and show-jumping events at several places, such as Boston. **The Lincoln Half Marathon** has in the past taken place in early May, with the **Lincoln Grand Prix Cycle Race** later in the same month. The annual **Milk Race** comes through Lincoln too, of course, in early June. Another very testing sporting event is the **Lincoln to Boston Rowing Marathon**, which takes place in mid-September. For details of all these and other sporting events, contact local TICs.

Cultural events have their place too, of course, and among the most important are the **Lincoln Mystery Plays**, performed in Lincoln Cathedral in July. At around the same time there is also the **Lincoln Castle Medieval Fayre** - but if you want this type of entertainment and are not in Lincoln at just the right time, do not despair. There are regular **jousting tournaments held at Belvoir Castle**, where a really busy and imaginative season of entertainment may include anything from handbell ringing to displays of falconry, from country dancing to historic vehicle rallies, and from displays of archery to Morris men.

From medieval fairs to **Steam Fairs**, which bring a festival atmosphere from a somewhat later age; several of these take place in the region throughout the summer and are usually most enjoyable events, with fairground organs as well as old vehicles, threshing machines, old tractors and so on.

Arts and crafts are flourishing in the area too. There is a busy programme of musical and artistic events throughout the year, at such venues as the **Usher Hall** in Lincoln and **Lincoln Theatre Royal**. Lincoln has its own **Art Festival** in early May, preceded by South Holland's, from mid-April to mid-May and followed by Stamford's at the end of May. Festivals of **Country Music** have been held in the region too, as well as a **Jazz Bands** Championship in Skegness in August. For details of these and similar events, enquire at TICs.

Craft fairs will be found throughout the region and are certainly too numerous to list here. They are most enjoyable to visit, however, and there is always the chance that you will pick up some real treasure that will remind you of your holiday here for ever after.

Finally, we can't leave this marvellously busy County without mentioning flower festivals. The most famous is the **Spalding Flower Parade and Festival** in early May, but numerous other towns and villages have similar events, usually held in early summer. And if all this leaves you rather gasping for energy, what about the **Lincoln Wine Festival**, in June?

Leisure Activities in Lincolnshire

The opportunities for enjoying outdoor and sporting activities in Lincolnshire are more or less limitless. For full information, you should always contact TICs. A page such as this can only introduce a few of the possibilities. After that, in the next two pages, we feature four selected places to visit.

Walking is one of the most enjoyable and rewarding ways to discover the countryside and no county in Britain can be more assiduous and organised in documenting its walks than Lincolnshire. Lincolnshire County Council Recreation Services produce an almost bewildering number of **Lincolnshire Walks Leaflets**, distinctive in style and offering a huge range of possibilities to the keen walker. It is, of course, a `comfortable' county in which to walk, being so generally flat. Please note that a number of Walks and Drives are featured in this guide.

The flat countryside also favours other pursuits, such as **horse riding** and **cycling**. There are several riding schools and trekking centres in the region, and opportunities for hiring bicycles are on the increase, to answer the huge growth in popularity of this sport.

The vast network of waterways, both the rivers and the somewhat unattractively named `drains', offer limitless opportunities for boating. Parts of the River Witham, Foss Dyke (a canal that actually dates from Roman times) and the River Trent belong to the East Midlands Cruiseway - and these same waterways offer hours of entertainment to fishermen as well.

Water on a larger scale can be enjoyed at several locations, offering the chance to water-ski, jet-ski, windsurf and sail. The Castle Leisure Park at Tattershall, East Lincolnshire Marine in Ashby Park near Horncastle and Tallington Lakes Leisure Park near Stamford all offer at least some of these sports. And of course, not very far from Stamford is Rutland Water, one of the largest expanses of water in Europe available for recreational use.

All the standard sports can be enjoyed in the region, such as tennis, badminton, squash, bowls and golf (a particularly good course at Woodhall Spa). There are several **leisure centres** in the area, some with excellent **swimming pools**. Those at Stamford and Bourne (open air and heated) are good examples, as is the North Kesteven Sports Centre at North Hykeham. Meanwhile, what one might call more serious swimmers will look for a six lane, Olympic-style pool - and that can be found too, for instance at Grimsby.

If you prefer salt water, there are **excellent coastal resorts**, with a long tradition of supplying everything needed for a family holiday by the sea. The best known are Cleethorpes, Mablethorpe and Skegness, but smaller places like Sutton on Sea and Chapel St Leonards offer the quieter pleasures of seaside holiday too.

Animal Lovers will turn to the pages which detail attractions especially for them, and a list of **Country Parks and Nature Reserves** is given in the Directory at the end of this guide. But even then you have by no means exhausted the possibilities. You might like to seek out, for instance, the Fenside Goat Centre near Spilsby or the Butterfly Park near Holbeach, almost on the Wash.

Bird watching is very rewarding in this area, with the Gibraltar Point National Nature Reserve, also on the banks of the Wash, south of Skegness, being an especially good place from which to see the multitudes of wading birds which enjoy the rich pickings of the mudflats.

Not all the best wildlife sites are on the coast, however. **Snipe Dales** in the southern Wolds, featured as one of the Walks in this guide, is a delightful area to explore, being quiet and unspoilt. It is odd to reflect that one of the important Battles of the Civil War was fought here in 1643. In the Battle of Winceby, the Royalist forces of the Marquis of Newcastle were severely beaten by the Parliamentarians, under Sir Thomas Fairfax and Oliver Cromwell.

Finally, the towns have plenty to offer too. There are several good **town walks**, again well documented and sometimes escorted by a guide. Lincoln itself, for instance, is well supplied with parks and gardens, including Hartsholme Country Park, Boultham Park and the Monks Wood Arboretum, not to mention the vast West and South Commons. And Woodhall Spa also has an excellent park, as well as the unexpected Kinema in the Woods. As we said at the beginning, the opportunities for enjoying outdoor leisure pursuits in Lincolnshire are more or less limitless!

The towns and villages of this green English county display a quaint and colourful aspect to their character

St Botolph's Church, well-known as Boston Stump, looks over Boston's busy market place (BBC)

The thriving and popular town of Spalding is famous throughout the land for its brightly coloured fields of flowers (SHDC)

The picturesque riverside setting of Welland Terrace is just one example of the many fine buildings along the River Welland in Spalding (SHDC)

The White Horse Inn in Spalding is a quaint old building with a tremendous thatched roof (SHDC)

Beside the peaceful waters the lazily drooping willows set the mood for relaxation (SHDC)

This narrow country road near Somersby is certainly well away from the hustle and bustle of modern living (LCC)

One of the many pretty country lanes to be found in the Lincolnshire Wolds (LCC)

The romantic glades at Hubbard's Hill near Louth (LCC)

The country lanes and riverside walks of Lincolnshire typify the very best of rural England

Tattershall Park Country Club

Tattershall, Lincolnshire
Tel: (0526) 43193

The ideal Family Camping and Caravanning Site incorporating - Lakes, Woodland and Parkland in a 365 acre complex Caravans & Log Cabins available for sale and for hire.

SOMETHING FOR ALL THE FAMILY

Windsurfing, Water Ski-ing, Jet-Ski, Canoeing, Rowing, Pedalo, Horse Riding, Pony Trekking, Squash, Snooker Room, Gymnasium, Saunas and Solarium. Coarse Fishing, Fly Fishing, Island Adventure Playground, Restaurants, Bars, Camp Shop. Situated on the A153 Sleaford to Skegness Road

DAY VISITORS WELCOME

Blaydon Guest House
24 Scotgate
Stamford
Lincolnshire
PE9 2YQ.

Tel: 0780 62032

"An enchanting summer's evening..."

Stamford Shakespeare Company
ANNUAL SUMMER SEASONS OF SHAKESPEARE PLAYS

Seasons run June and July to mid August

Rutland Open Air Theatre, *(Covered Auditorium)*
Tolethorpe Hall, Stamford, Lincolnshire
(Just off A1)

1991 Season: June 14 to August 24...
Henry V · Twelfth Night
Much Ado About Nothing

(1991 Sponsors: Leicester Printers & Calor Gas)

BOOKING OFFICE (Open May to August)
TELEPHONE: 0780 56133 *(10 - 4 daily)*

COLOUR BROCHURE from Libraries, Tourist Information Centres and Arts Centres or send 9 x 4 sae **NOW** to Stamford Shakespeare Co. at the above address.

Bar, restaurant, ample car and coach parking. Advance booking essential.

General Enquiries: 0780 54381

Tolethorpe... it's magical!

Selected Leisure Activities

Tattershall Park Country Club is a superb family holiday and leisure centre set in 148 hectares (365 acres) of woods, lakes and parkland in the heart of Lincolnshire. Horse-riding, water-skiing and wind-surfing are available to the accomplished sportsman, whilst instruction for the beginner can be arranged for these three sports from fully qualified instructors. Pony trekking, jet-ski, canoeing, rowing, coarse and fly fishing, lake swimming from the man-made sandy beach and an Island Adventure Playground can also be enjoyed by day visitors, as well as caravanners and campers.

The Main Building comprises Squash Courts, Gymnasium, Saunas, Mallard Bar and Restaurant, Teal Bar and Snooker Room plus changing rooms, showers and toilet facilities. There is also a separate Camp Shop providing a wide range of goods. One, two, three or four-mile **Nature Walks** can be followed within the park and no less than 75 different varieties of birds have been identified.

Two and three bedroom holiday homes are available for sale or hire and over 300 caravan and tenting pitches are available on a season-ticket, short-term or a daily basis, on a choice of nine sites within the complex. These are served by three toilet and shower blocks plus toilets, showers and changing facilities in the Main Building. Further details of all the facilities at Tattershall Park are available from the Reception Office.

Stamford Shakespeare Company

Rutland Open Air Theatre lies in an idyllic wooded glen in a natural amphitheatre in the grounds of Elizabethan Tolethorpe Hall, just off the A1 near Stamford. This largely undiscovered corner of South Lincolnshire is the home of the **Stamford Shakespeare Company**, who annually present one of the most successful open air summer Shakespeare seasons outside London.

The Theatre is the only open air theatre with a covered auditorium, having comfortable amphitheatre-style seating beneath a canvas canopy, while the stage is in the open air, set among huge trees and shrubs. Indeed, no performance has ever been cancelled or even halted because of inclement weather! Although an amateur company, the Stamford Shakespeare Company has a reputation for professional standards both on and off the stage, priding itself on spectacular sets and beautiful costumes.

Visitors are welcomed by car park attendants in cricket umpire jackets, and then make their way through the beautiful gardens to **Tolethorpe Hall.** A special pathway has been created for disabled visitors in wheelchairs. In front of the Hall are spacious lawns edged by a low C16th wall and beautifully set off by beds of Elizabethan roses (Rosa Mundi). On the ground floor of Tolethorpe Hall are two spacious and well appointed restaurants, where an excellent cold buffet is served, along with a fine choice of wines. The spacious bar opens through French windows directly on to the lawn. Beyond is a large sloping area of grass where, on hot summer evenings, patrons enjoy champagne picnics before the performance - at 8pm Monday to Thursday, and 9pm Friday and Saturday.

The company purchased Tolethorpe Hall as a derelict property in 1977, after nine successful years performing summer Shakespeare in the Monastery Garden of Stamford's historic George Hotel, and are thus able to stage a 10 week summer season, attracting up to 23,000 patrons, with most evenings almost sold out often weeks in advance. Many patrons are prepared to travel up to two hours to spend an evening at Tolethorpe - which has deservedly earned the description of being 'magical'.

Promoted abroad by the East Midlands Tourist Board, the Theatre now also attracts an increasing number of overseas tourists each year. Keen Shakespeare fans book for both Friday and Saturday night performances for a holiday weekend, staying in one of the many low price private guest houses in the area, a list of which can be obtained from the TIC, the Museum, Broad Street, Stamford.

Postal bookings start from March 1st annually and the Box Office opens for telephone bookings from around May 1st - it is advisable to book early. For details, please send a stamped addressed envelope (9x4) to the Stamford Shakespeare Company, Tolethorpe Hall, nr Stamford, PE9 4BH. General Inquiries, Tel: 0780 54381. Box Office (open 10am-4pm, daily from May 1st to August 24th), Tel: 0780 56133.

The very precise craft of wood-turning can be marvelled at in Newgates Gallery, Stamford (NG)

A fascinating view of the interior of Rutland Cottage Music and Fairground Museum in Whaplode St Catherines near Spalding (RC)

A splendid display of the finished products on view at Newgates Gallery (NG)

Working craftsmen, museums and a host of wildlife attractions are just a few of Lincolnshire's countless treasures

A blue and gold macaw getting up to all sorts of antics at The Animal Gardens at North End, Mablethorpe (AG)

Natureland Seal Sanctuary at Skegness is very popular with children who love to see the baby seals (NSS)

Jungle World at Cleethorpes offers a variety of wildlife for your pleasure, such as this very brightly coloured butterfly (JW)

The cells at Boston Guildhall Museum, where the early Pilgrim Fathers were imprisoned (BBC)

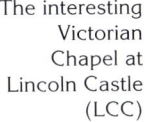

The interesting Victorian Chapel at Lincoln Castle (LCC)

The peaceful countryside setting of Tolethorpe Hall is very appropriate for its role as home of the Stamford Shakespeare Company (SSC)

There are so many varied and interesting places to visit in this magnificent English county

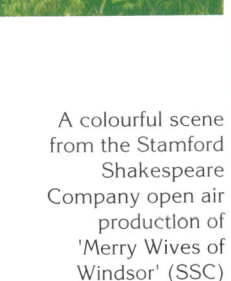

A colourful scene from the Stamford Shakespeare Company open air production of 'Merry Wives of Windsor' (SSC)

RIVER TRIPS
WITH LOCK & CASTLE LINE

Public Trips are run most weekends from Easter to the end of October plus most weekdays during peak periods. Private Trips are available throughout the Summer Season. Business Parties, Schools, Disabled Parties, Clubs, Groups and Family Celebrations are all welcome. We can provide full bar facilities and a varied menu if required. Drinks and snacks are always available. We are a family business offering a personal service and staff who take a pride in their work.

For further details phone Newark (0636) 707939

DEPARTING FROM TOWN WHARF NEWARK-ON-TRENT

Enjoy the Elsham Experience

Park Open Everyday
**Easter to October
11am to 5pm**
New Falconry Centre
New Craft Centre
New Granary Restaurant
Hot Meals & Sunday Lunch available
Details (0652) 688698
Elsham Hall Country Park Brigg
(8 miles south from the Humber Bridge.)

Lock and Castle Line River Trips

Lock and Castle Line operate **River Trips** from Newark on Trent, leaving from the Town Wharf, which is situated below the impressive Ossington Hotel. Here you can take a river trip, relaxing and enjoying the peace and tranquillity of England's third longest river, with its townscapes, wildlife and country meadows. **Newark** has a varied array of riverside buildings, from the C12th Castle to C20th dwellings. In the course of the journey, one also experiences a lock where the river changes level by two metres. Meanwhile, the River Trent is renowned for its fishing and is also an ideal venue for the budding ornithologist, with a wide range of birds to be discovered - including the majestic heron and the elusive kingfisher.

Lock and Castle Line's passenger boats are designed to enable visitors to enjoy a trip regardless of the weather. All the boats meet the rigorous Department of Trade and Industry standards and comply with their regulations. On board the sixty seater boats, visibility is excellent. There is a good cup of tea or coffee available (in real cups and saucers!) or something from the bar if preferred. The majority of **public trips** are 65 minutes long but a variety of trips are often offered at weekends (see 'River Cruise').

Private bookings are a speciality. Women's Institutes, senior citizens' groups, schools, disabled parties, clubs and family celebrations are all welcome. A varied menu is offered and bar facilities are available if required. Daytime bookings can be any length from one hour upwards. Evening bookings are two or three hours long.

Lock and Castle Line is a family business offering a relaxing trip in pleasant surroundings and staff who take a pride in their work - certainly a trip worth discovering.

Elsham Hall Country Park

Elsham Hall Country Park's lovely wooded grounds near Brigg, South Humberside, offer the visitor a whole world of discovery. The park occupies the beautiful grounds of **Elsham Hall**, which contain three lakes, round which grows a wonderful variety of shrubs and spring flowers. It was opened to the public in 1970 by the owners, Mr and Mrs Elwes, so that members of the public could explore the 160 hectares (400 acres) of grounds and at the same time enjoy discovering more about the local wildlife.

Nature Trails wander through the Estate and trail leaflets are available, while on some Sundays and Bank Holidays guided walks are taken by the warden. Other areas to explore include the **Monks Wood Arboretum**, whose wide range of British native and forestry trees are now a decade old, and the **Hazel Coppice Bird Garden**, full of free-flying native and foreign birds. There is also a **Wild Butterfly Garden**, best appreciated in the autumn, when the various butterflies and moths are at their most numerous. The walkway through this garden won a special award in 1987.

A new feature is a **Falconry Centre**, where demonstrations are given at 2pm, while the **Walled Garden** contains domestic animals, including rare breeds of livestock, poultry and pheasants. The **Animal Farm**, meanwhile, gives children a chance to see something of how a farm is run (milking demonstrations, lambing etc.) and meet typical farmyard animals. Immediately adjacent is the **Adventure Playground**, where any surplus energy can soon be happily burnt off.

Fishermen will enjoy trying out their skills on the **Trout Lake**. Season permits are available by arrangement with the fishing syndicate and those interested should apply to the Estate Office. Meanwhile, those who prefer to see fish but not catch them will enjoy the **Carp Lake**, where the fish can be fed (food available in the Shop) from a special platform.

There is also the **Wrawby Moor Art Gallery**, a range of craft workshops and **Elsham Forge**, which is open on Sundays and Bank Holidays, when local blacksmith Harry Lindsey is present. The skills of a metalworker in a slightly different idiom are on display in the **Brass Rubbing Centre**, where you can make your own rubbings of endangered British species. Add to this a gift shop, tea room and restaurant, along with conference, wedding and caravanning facilities, and you have the ingredients for a perfect day out. The Park is open daily during summer, 11am to 5pm and Sundays in winter. For further details Tel: (0652) 688698.

A most magnificent sunset over The Wash (SHDC)

Just a small part of the extensive Lincolnshire coastline awaiting your enjoyment (LCC)

The beautiful coastline and countryside of Lincolnshire have contributed to its way of life and rich heritage

The region's maritime heritage can be experienced at the National Fishing Heritage Centre at Grimsby (GBC)

A very impressive view of the front of Stamford Steam Brewery Museum with an old dray in the foreground (SSBM)

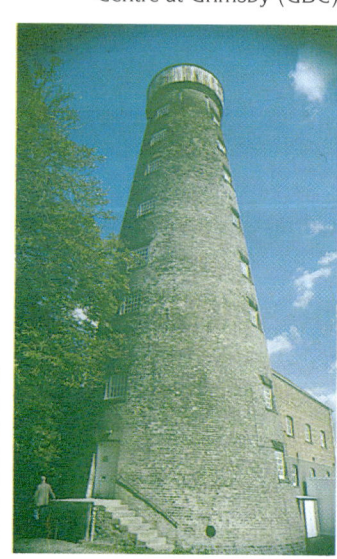

Another of the County's many very interesting historic buildings (SHDC)

Another peaceful countryside scene showing the rural way of life (LCC)

The golden cornfields add a richness and colour to the canvas of Lincolnshire (LCC)

A panoramic view over Tetford and the rural farming landscape of East Lincolnshire (LCC)

Large parts of the region are extremely flat with views extending for miles across unspoilt, productive farmland (LCC)

The spectacular eight-sailed Heckington Windmill (NKDC)

Windmills are one of the integral characteristics of the personality of this extensive farming region

Windmills in Lincolnshire

Water and wind have been used to drive mills for centuries, possibly since the Romans. Mills certainly existed by the time of the Domesday Book, which mentioned 200 watermills in Lincolnshire, and there were possibly as many as 700 and there by the C12th. Mill enthusiasts have formed the 'Lincolnshire Mills Group' (including Humberside and Nottinghamshire) 'to preserve and promote the milling heritage of the region'.

ALFORD MILL In 1837 Alford had its own millwright, Mr. Sam Oxley, who built this mill which was bought by Lincolnshire County Council in 1955, at the end of its commercial life, and renovated. At the time of the Alford Festival, Bank Holidays and Saturdays (March to Sept.), it can be seen at work. Alford is on the A1104.

ALVINGHAM MILL on the River Lud near Louth. There has been a mill here since 1155. Today's mill has survived since the C18th. Water entering a wheel can either fall into paddles (over-shot mill) or hit the paddles of the wheel underneath (under-shot mill), but Alvingham is unusual in that the water enters the paddles of the wheel on a line with the axle. This is called a breast-wheel. Restored and in working order, it can be visited on selected days from Easter to the end of August.

BURGH LE MARSH MILL A five storey mill built by Sam Oxley in 1813. Sometimes known as Dobson's Mill, it was purchased by Lincolnshire County Council and restored. The curious thing about this mill is the 5 left handed sails, which therefore rotate anti-clockwise. It opens every second and last Sunday in the month. Burgh le Marsh is outside Skegness on the Lincoln road, A158.

CLAYTHORPE MILL Off the B1373 at Withern near South Thoresby. Originally C18th and in lovely surroundings, it is open to the public (with a craft shop and tea-rooms) daily in spring and summer, weekends only in autumn and winter.

ELLIS MILL Lincoln. This mill affords marvellous views across the countryside. As its address, Mill Road, suggests it was at one time one of many in the vicinity. Lincoln Civic Trust has restored this remaining 4-sailed tower mill, and, wind permitting, it grinds at the weekends.

MAUD FOSTER MILL This 5-sailed mill stands proud on the edge of Boston and you can climb all of its 7 storeys and purchase delicacies from the whole food shop.

SIBSEY TRADER MILL On the B1184 west of the village. This six-sailed mill was built by another Lincolnshire millwright, Saunderson of Louth, in 1877. It was working commercially until the late 1950s, was later restored and now opens to the public most days in the summer.

STOCKWITH MILL In a lovely peaceful spot in Tennyson Country, between Hagworthingham and Harrington, this is an undershot water-mill, sadly no longer in working order but used today as a tea room and craft centre. Off A158, March to Dec. 10.30am to 6pm Closed Monday, except Bank Holidays.

TEALBY THORPE MILL Another beautiful water mill on a site where a mill has probably stood for a thousand years.

WALTHAM MILL A tower mill with 6 sails. After considerable restoration, it is open on Sunday afternoons in the summer. Waltham is south of Grimsby on the B1203.

WRAWBY MILL This last remaining post mill in the north of England, has 4 sails and stoneground flour is sold here. Travelling through Wrawby in the Brigg direction on the A18 it can be found down a little lane on the left. It is open on selected days.

Heckington Mill

The village of Heckington, in an area of rich agricultural land on the edge of the Fens, is the proud possessor of a unique eight-sailed windmill. Originally built as a five-sailer in 1830, Heckington Mill was tailwinded by a violent thunderstorm in 1890, which blew off the cap and sails. The Nash family, who owned the Mill, sold it to John Pocklington in 1891. Using the cap and sails from Skirbeck Mill in Boston, John Pocklington restored the Mill as an eight-sailer with the help of a local millwright early in 1892.

The Mill continued to work until shortly after John Pocklington's death in 1941. The shutters were removed soon after it stopped work. Idle, the Mill soon deteriorated until bought by Kesteven County Council in 1953, when it was made safe. Following extensive repairs, including a new cap and lightning conductor, the Mill has been restored to full working order and is now in the ownership of Lincolnshire County Council.

The Friends of Heckington Mill work with the owners to care for the Mill and keep alive the traditional milling skills. The Mill is open daily to the public and can be seen working, wind permitting, at weekends. You can also visit the Windmill Shop in the Pearoom Craft Centre (see 'Crafts'), just across from the Mill.

Famous People

It is always interesting to see if there appear to be any links between the famous people of one area - but Lincolnshire's celebrities seem especially varied and among them no easily discernible pattern is seen.

Starting from the earliest days, we find **Hereward The Wake**, whose birthplace was the settlement of Bourne. His exact dates are unknown but he is recorded as a major Lincolnshire land-owner in the Domesday Book. In 1070, he led an uprising of the native English against the invading Normans at Ely, and then, assisted by Danish invaders, attacked Peterborough in the same year. When his allies surrendered to William the Conqueror, he escaped, but he was eventually killed by the Normans in France.

Another important figure from the Norman period is **Saint Hugh of Lincoln** - but here we run into immediate danger of confusion, because there have, in fact, been **two Saints of Lincoln named Hugh**. The earlier, known as **Hugh of Avalon**, lived from about 1135 to the year 1200. Having been trained as a monk in the Grande Chartreuse monastery in France, he came to England at the invitation of Henry II in 1175 and became Bishop of Lincoln in 1186. He was known for his unimpeachable character and his mistrust of so-called miracles - and he was responsible for the rebuilding of Lincoln Cathedral, devastated first by fire and then an earthquake, in Early English style, making it eventually one of the most splendid in the country.

The other St Hugh was an unfortunate child of about eight or nine years, said to have been starved, tortured and crucified in Lincoln by a Jew named Copin in 1255. His place of burial in the Cathedral, near that of another famous bishop, **Bishop Grosseteste**, became much venerated by pilgrims.

Henry IV was born at Bolingbroke, where there is still a castle to this day, in 1367. This first Plantagenet King is brilliantly portrayed in Shakespeare's 'Richard II.' The haughty Richard, his cousin, died in prison at Pontefract Castle in 1400, having been forced to cede the Crown to Henry in the previous year. Another Richard, often known as 'Saint' Richard Scrope, Archbishop of York, also died at Henry's hands in 1405, when he was executed for leading an uprising against the king, and the two deaths made Henry increasingly unpopular. He himself died in 1413.

John Cotton of Boston, a Puritan vicar, became famous for leading some three hundred **'Pilgrim Fathers'** across the Atlantic to the namesake town in Massachusetts, USA, in 1630. Prior to this successful departure, they had been imprisoned at the Boston Guildhall, where the Museum now tells their story.

Sir Isaac Newton, the famous scientist and mathematician, was born at Woolsthorpe Manor and attended school in Grantham, where the Museum has in important display about him. Remembered most for his discovery of the principle of gravity, he in fact wrote on many other matters, both scientific and theological, and his behaviour was apparently that of the typical 'absent minded professor.' Another famous figure from Grantham, of course, is **Margaret Thatcher**, former British Prime Minister, who is also featured in displays at the Museum.

Two famous explorers came from the region, **Matthew Flinders** (1777-1814), who was born at Donington and who was the first to explore much of the coastline of Australia; and **Sir John Franklin** (1786 - 1847), born at Spilsby, who had learnt some of his skills from Flinders and who then became an Arctic explorer. According to a note found with some abandoned boats in the North West Passage in Canada, he and his companions died after being trapped in the ice for some nineteen months - but he remains credited with having been the discoverer of the North West Passage all the same.

The poet, **Alfred, Lord Tennyson**, was born at Somersby, where his father was Rector, in 1809 and went to school in Louth. Among his best known poems are 'In Memoriam, 'The Charge of the Light Brigade', 'Maud' (slated by the critics at the time!) and 'Idylls of the King.' He succeeded Wordsworth as Poet Laureate in 1850 and died in 1892.

Lastly, there is just room to mention the monumental **Daniel Lambert** (1770-1809), still holding his place in the Guinness Book of Records as 'the most corpulent man of whom authentic record exists.' When he died he weighed nearly 53 stone (over 840 lbs) and is buried in St Martin's Churchyard, Stamford, where the local Museum has a feature about him. Finally, if anyone knows who the 'Lincolnshire Poacher' actually was, please let us know!

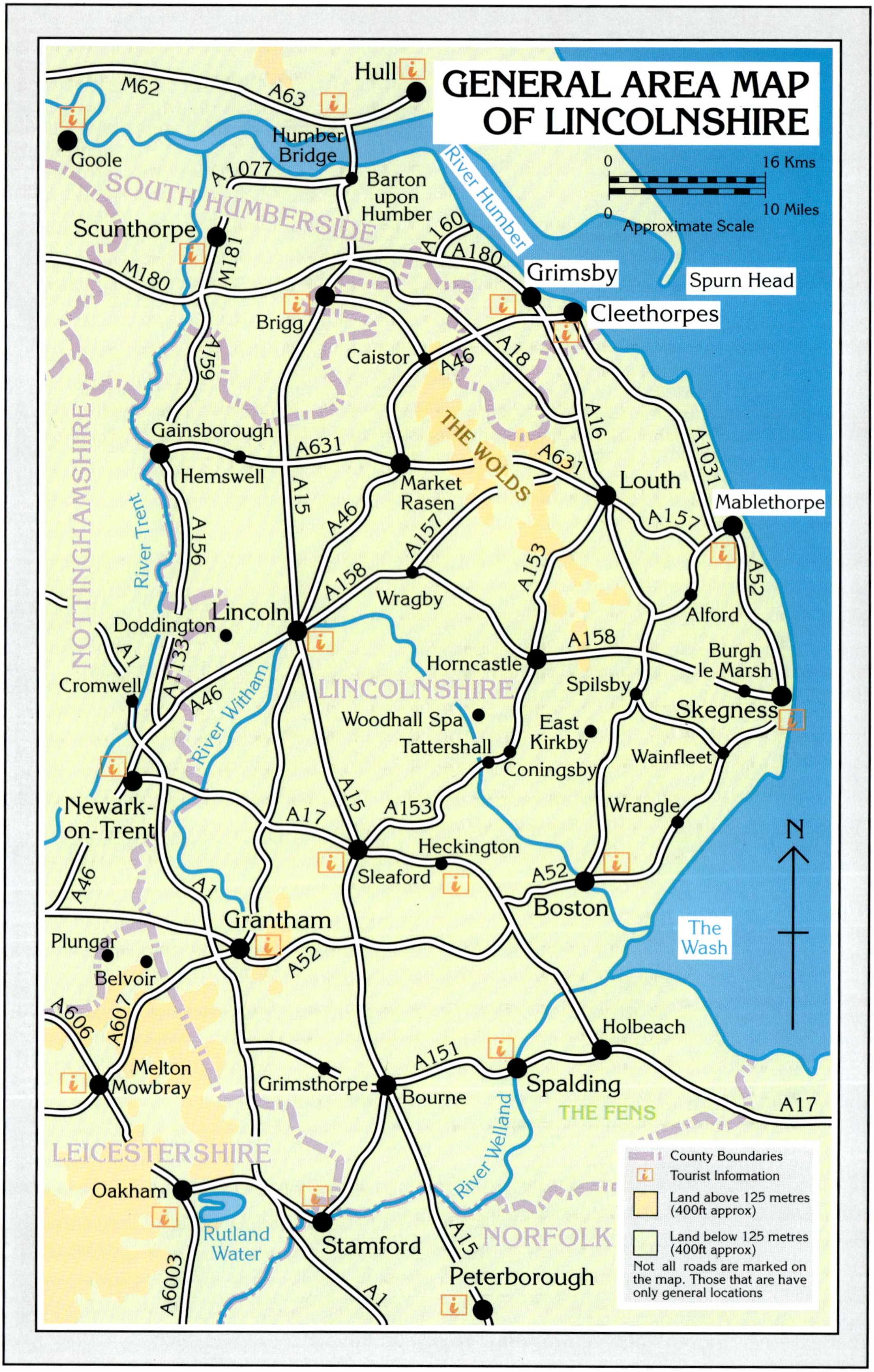
GENERAL AREA MAP OF LINCOLNSHIRE
0
16 Kms
0
10 Miles
Approximate Scale
Hull
M62
A63
Goole
Humber Bridge
Barton upon Humber
A1077
SOUTH HUMBERSIDE
River Humber
Scunthorpe
M181
M180
A160
A180
Grimsby
Spurn Head
Cleethorpes
Brigg
Caistor
A46
A18
A159
THE WOLDS
A16
A1031
Gainsborough
Hemswell
A631
Market Rasen
A631
Louth
Mablethorpe
A157
NOTTINGHAMSHIRE
River Trent
A156
A15
A46
A157
A153
A52
Wragby
A158
Alford
Doddington
Lincoln
A158
Burgh le Marsh
A1
A1133
Horncastle
Cromwell
LINCOLNSHIRE
Spilsby
Skegness
A46
River Witham
Woodhall Spa
East Kirkby
Tattershall
Wainfleet
Coningsby
Newark-on-Trent
A153
A15
A17
Wrangle
N
Heckington
A46
Sleaford
A52
A1
Boston
Grantham
The Wash
Plungar
Belvoir
A52
A606
A607
Holbeach
Melton Mowbray
A151
Grimsthorpe
Bourne
Spalding
THE FENS
A17
River Welland
LEICESTERSHIRE
Oakham
Rutland Water
Stamford
A15
NORFOLK
A6003
A1
Peterborough
County Boundaries
Tourist Information
Land above 125 metres (400ft approx)
Land below 125 metres (400ft approx)
Not all roads are marked on the map. Those that are have only general locations

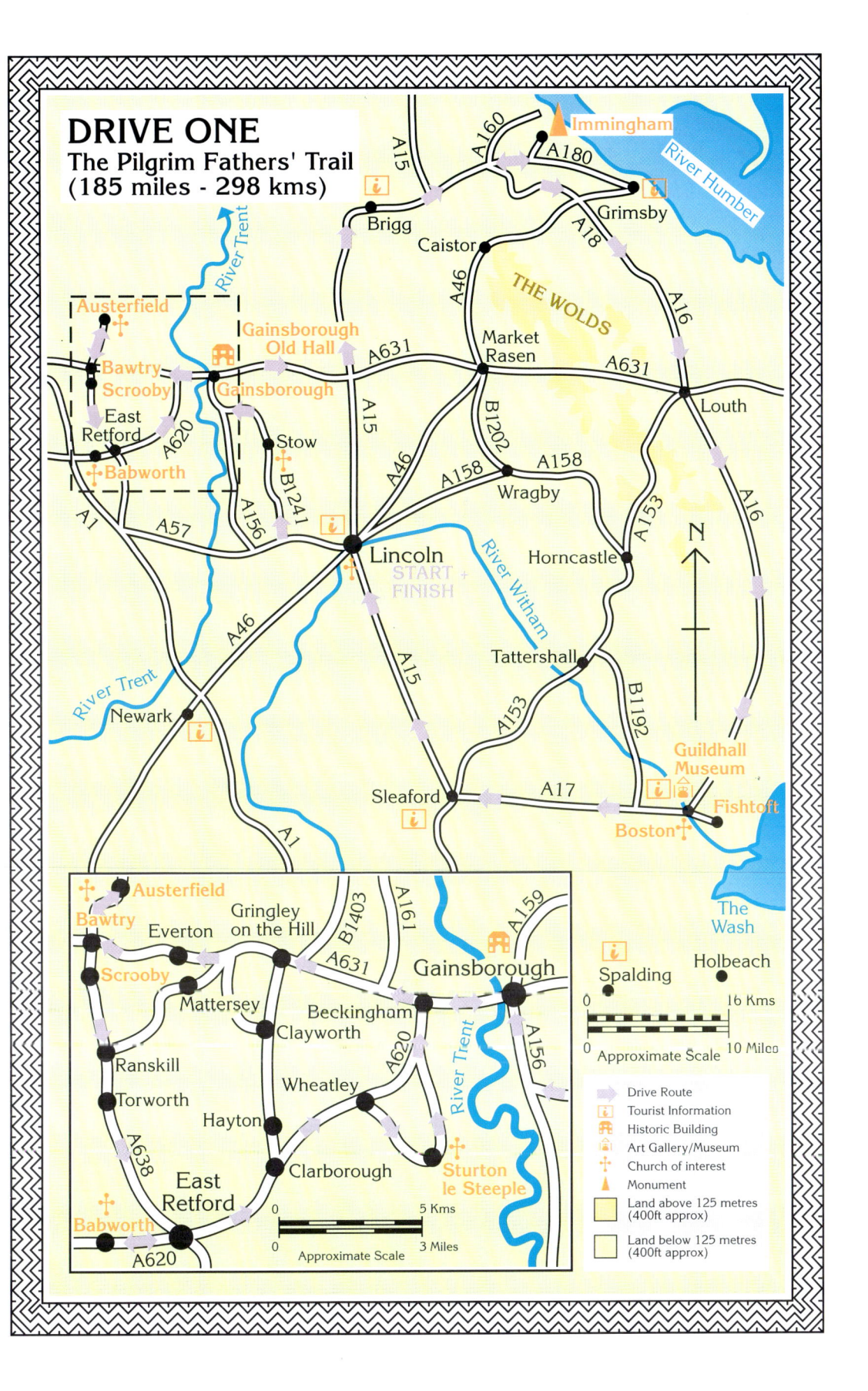

DRIVE ONE
The Pilgrim Fathers' Trail
(185 miles - 298 kms)

Drive One - Following the Pilgrim Fathers 52

Route: Lincoln, Stow, Gainsborough, Austerfield, Bawtry, Scrooby, Babworth, Sturton-le-Steeple, Gainsborough, Brigg, Immingham, Louth, Horncastle, Boston, Fishtoft, Boston, Sleaford, Lincoln

Distance: 185 miles - 282 kms approx.

General Description: It is no exaggeration to say that the small band of people who left this part of England, to sail to America and found a new, free religion, effectively changed the course of world history. This trail visits some of the places connected with these **'Pilgrim Fathers'**, from the small area in which they met and developed their ideas, to the coast, from which they departed their homeland for good.

Access: Lincoln is the start and finish point for this route, but the north-west reaches of the route lie very near the A1, and can thus be joined via either the A631 or the A620.

Route Instructions: Lincoln is an appropriate starting point for this route, as it was the **Bishop of Lincoln** who had to deal with the dissenting clergy and congregations in his diocese, as the Separatist movement developed in the early years of the C17th. **Lincoln Cathedral** is, of course, one of the most important landmarks in the entire County, but at that date the nearby **Bishop's Palace**, now a ruin, was also in use (it was destroyed in the Civil War in 1648).

Lincoln Castle, meanwhile, was a place of imprisonment for the Separatists after their abortive first attempt to leave from Boston. Leave Lincoln by the B1241 through **Stow**, whose Saxon Church of St Mary is the oldest church in Lincolnshire, and continue to Gainsborough.

Here, turn left on the A631 - but before reaching Bawtry, take a minor road to your right, to **Austerfield, birthplace of William Bradford**, who was baptised in the local church in 1590. As a young man, well read in theology and largely self-taught, Bradford joined the Scrooby congregation and was much influenced by the simple form of worship practised there. Much later, despite his humble beginnings, he became Governor of Plymouth Plantation in America, from 1621-1657. Now follow signs to Bawtry, where you cross the A631, and continue to Scrooby. **William Brewster**, who went to the University of Cambridge in 1580, before returning to live at **Scrooby Manor**, was a pivotal figure in the development of the Separatist movement. He offered sanctuary to **Richard Clyfton**, when the latter was deprived of his living at Babworth for his non-conformist views, and also welcomed the much younger William Bradford. The Manor House thus became an important meeting place for the members of the Scrooby congregation.

Now continue to Retford and turn right for a short distance on the A620 to **Babworth**, where Richard Clyfton preached so influentially. Now retrace your route along the A620, this time continuing through Retford and Clarborough to Wheatley, where you can make a brief detour to the right to **Sturton le Steeple, home of John Robinson,** another Cambridge graduate and clergyman with non-conformist sympathies. Now return to the A620, which meets the A631 at Beckingham, and turn right to Gainsborough. **William Hickman, of Gainsborough Old Hall** (open to the public), was another sympathiser who regularly welcomed members of the Separatist movement to his home, where the local pastor, **John Smyth**, was another powerful influence. Constantly persecuted for their beliefs, the group eventually decided to leave for Holland, where there was greater religious freedom - but King James I, who had declared in 1604, 'I will make them conform or I will harry them out of the land', refused to allow them to leave.

Now take the A631 east to the junction with the A15, turn left to Brigg and then follow the A180 to **Immingham**. Here, a monument opposite the Church commemorates those Pilgrims who did manage to escape to Holland in 1608. Others had tried unsuccessfully to leave from Boston in the previous year, but were betrayed by their captain; and **Boston** is the next destination on this trail, reached by means of the A16 across the Wolds, through Louth and Spilsby. Here, you can see the **Guildhall's** displays on the Pilgrim Fathers and the cells where they were temporarily imprisoned, before their successful departure in 1608.

From here, the trail leaves England, therefore, strictly speaking from the little port of Fishtoft, and proceeds to Amsterdam, then to Leyden and finally, when conditions for non-conformists became less comfortable in Holland, to **Boston, Massachusetts**, in America. We, however, take the A17 west from Boston to Sleaford and then the A15 back to Lincoln.

Drives Two and Three - Two Craft Trails

Route 1: Lincoln, Metheringham, Martin, Woodhall Spa, Coningsby, New York, Frithville, Sibsey, Wrangle, Wainfleet, Irby in the Marsh, Alford, Louth, Market Rasen, Waddingham, Hemswell, Scampton, Lincoln

Distance: 114 miles - 183 kms

Access: This route could best be joined from Lincoln or Louth.

General Description: A varied route which travels through the Fen country most of the way to the coast and then turns north to travel back to Lincoln across the Wolds.

Route Instructions: After visiting **Cobb Hall Crafts** in Lincoln's ancient Bailgate, take the B1188 to Metheringham and then follow signs for Woodhall Spa. This means taking the B1189 and then the B1191 through the little village of Martin. Woodhall Spa is the home of **Grosvenor Manor** and the **Broadway Craft Centre**.

Now take the B1192 to Coningsby, through which you join the A153 before resuming the B1192 to New York, immediately after which you fork left on a true fen road to Frithville and join the B1184 to Sibsey, where there are two windmills, the Sibsey Trader Mill being the more notable. Continue to Wrangle, home of **Wrangle Pottery**, and up the A52 to Wainfleet.

Now turn inland again on the B1195 to Irby in the Marsh, at the end of which a right turn passes Gunby Hall and then comes to a major road junction, where you take the B1196 for Alford. Taking the A1104 north through Saleby, look out for the B1373 link (past Woodthorpe Hall Holiday Park) to the A157 and Louth.

Follow the A157 through the town and out the other side and then fork right on the A631 for a breezy drive across this famous racehorse training area of the Wolds to Market Rasen. Continue on the A631 until you are signed right to Waddingham. This will take you close to the **Brandy Wharf Cider Centre**, which is signed.

From Waddingham, take the B1205 west to cross the A15 (which is the Roman road, the Ermine Way) and then turn left on the B1398 to Hemswell, home of **Hemswell Antiques**. Rather than returning to the busy A15, continue south down the B1398 and back to Lincoln.

Route 2: Stamford, Dingle, Tallington, Spalding, Weston, Heckington, Sleaford, Leadenham, Fulbeck, Carlton Scroop, Abcaster, Oasby, Welby, Colsterworth, Stamford

Distance: 92 miles - 148 kms

Access: Stamford, Spalding and Sleaford are the main access points on this route, and Grantham would be another easy access point.

Route Instructions: Stamford has plenty to offer. Not only is it a very beautiful town, it is also the home of the **Newgates Gallery** (in Elm Street) and **Stamford Antiques** (in the Exchange Hall, Broad Street).

Leaving Stamford, however, by the B1443 past Burghley House, you make for the **Dingle Nursery** at Pilsgate, before continuing to Bainton, where you turn left for Tallington. Joining the A16 to the right, you now cross Deeping Fen to Spalding.

Leave Spalding on the A151 north east, past Springfields Gardens to Weston. **Bay Tree Nurseries** are found here, in High Road. After Weston take the B1357 north, which soon links up with the A17.

Follow this good road some 15 miles (24 kms) to Heckington, home of the most spectacular of all the Lincolnshire windmills. Here there is the **Pearoom Craft Centre**. Now continue on the A17 to by-pass Sleaford and pass RAF Cranwell, before reaching Leadenham.

Just south of Leadenham on the A607 is Fulbeck, where the Manor Stables Craft Workshops are found. Continue south on the A607 as far as Carlton Scroop, where you take a minor road to the left, signed to Ancaster through Sudbrook. Here you turn right on the B6403 (part of Roman Ermine Street) and shortly fork left on a minor road to Oasby, home of the **Oasby Pot Shop**.

From here, another minor road signed to Welby will lead you back to the B6403, where you can turn south to Colsterworth. You need to remain on this road and go underneath the A1, alongside the meandering River Witham and past Woolsthorpe Manor, home of Sir Isaac Newton, before you can join the A1 going south, which gives you a quick, if busy, run back to Stamford.

DRIVE TWO
CRAFT TRAIL (North)
(114 miles - 183 kms)

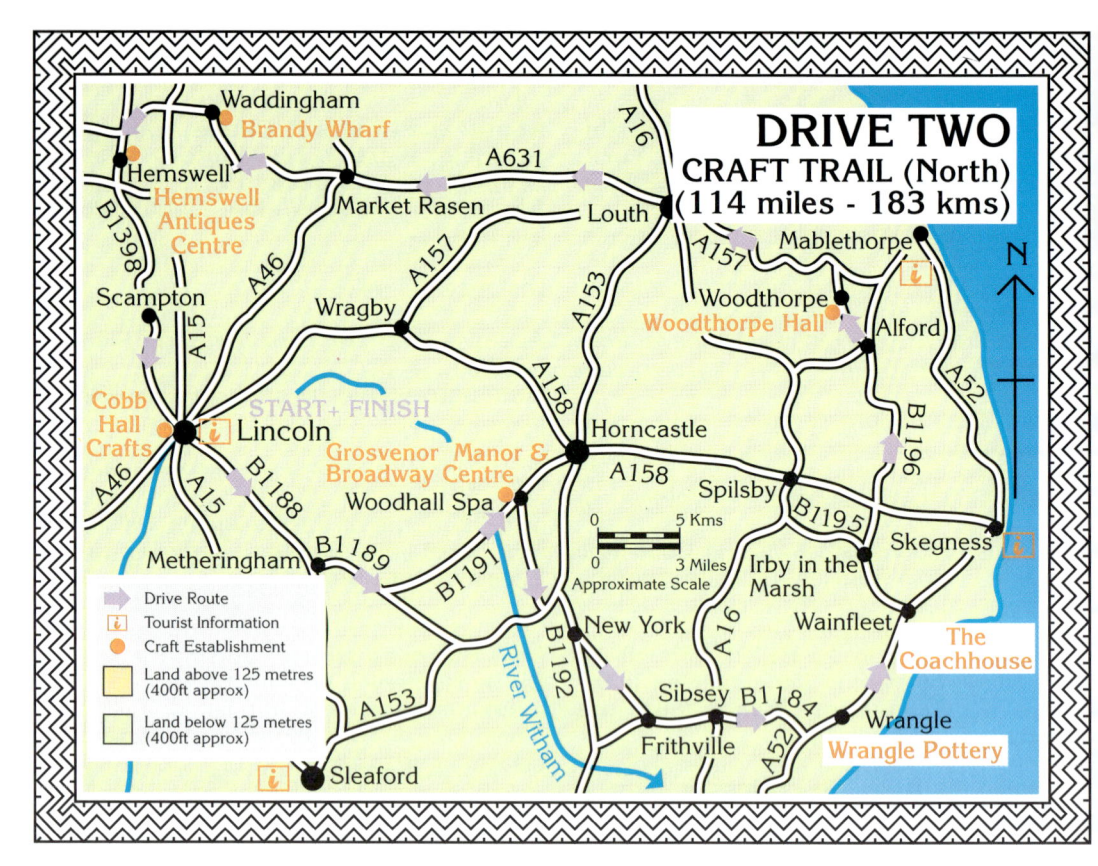

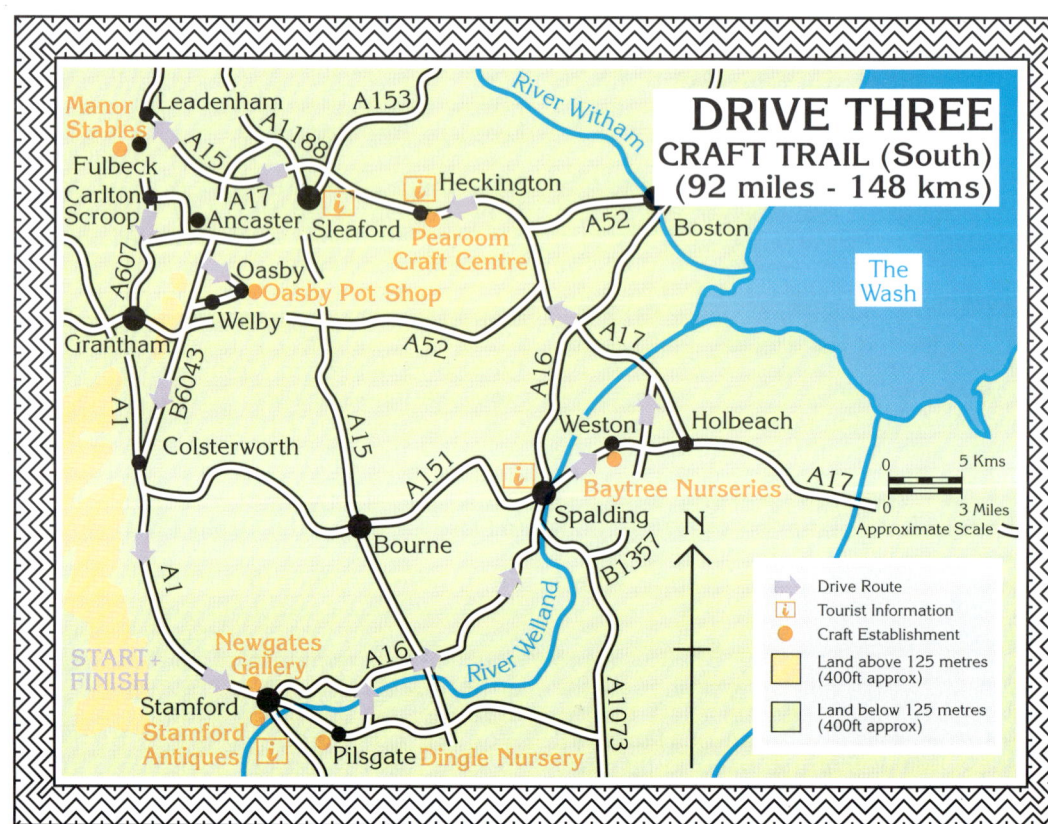

DRIVE THREE
CRAFT TRAIL (South)
(92 miles - 148 kms)

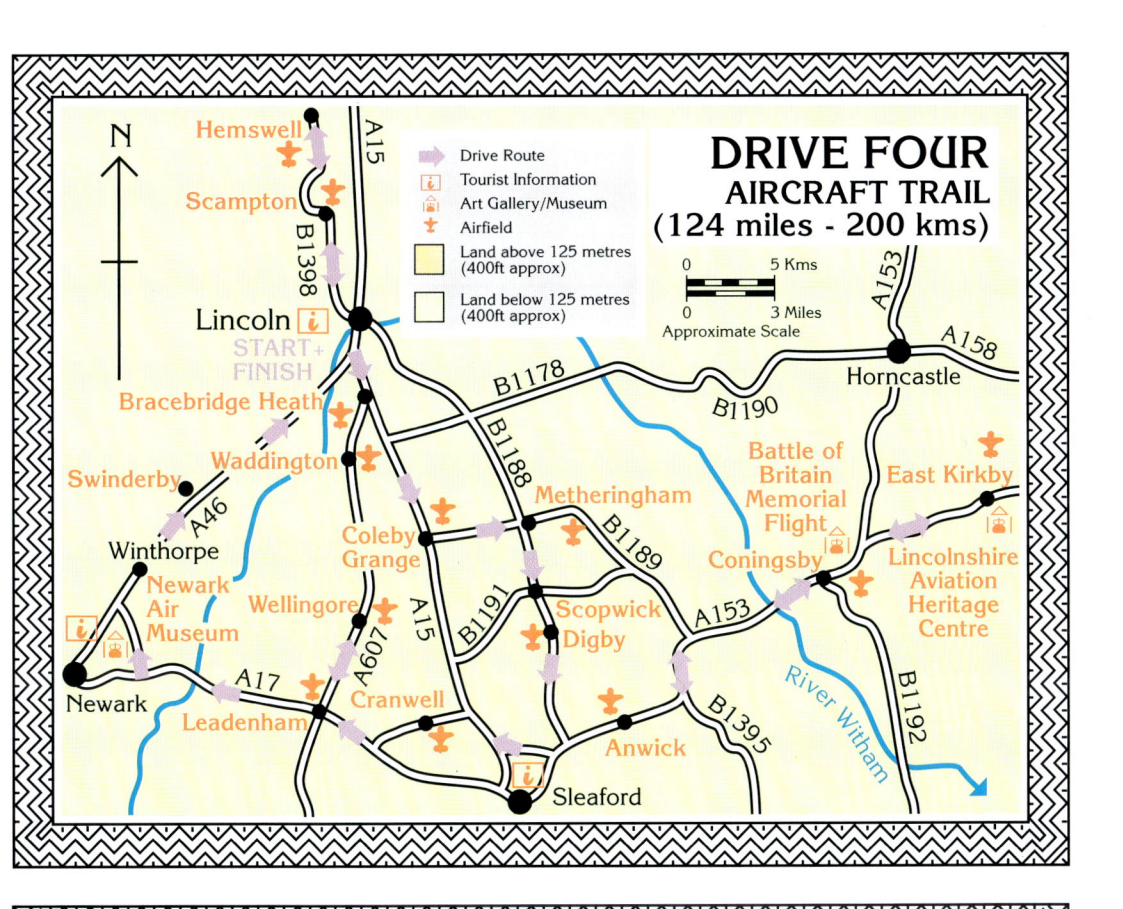

DRIVE FOUR
AIRCRAFT TRAIL
(124 miles - 200 kms)

DRIVE FIVE
WILDLIFE TRAIL
(89 miles - 143 kms)

Drive Four - for Aircraft Enthusiasts

Route: Lincoln, Bracebridge Heath, Waddington, Coleby Grange, Metheringham, Digby, Anwick, Coningsby (Battle of Britain Memorial Flight), East Kirkby (Lincolnshire Aviation Heritage Centre), Cranwell, Leadenham, Wellingore, Newark (Air Museum), Swinderby, Lincoln.

Distance: 124 miles - 200 kms including the additional detour in the last paragraph.

Route Instructions: You start from **Lincoln** itself, where the famous **Cathedral** is a landmark for miles around, both for those on the ground and in the air. One of Lincoln's pioneering engineering firms was Robey's, whose airstrip at **Bracebridge Heath** is the first place visited on this Trail. Next on the Trail is **RAF Waddington**, still an extensive airfield, whose main runway was built in 1953. Please note that for safety reasons no parking is allowed on either the carriageway or verges of the A15 to the east of Waddington Airfield.

From here you pass south along the A15, until the watch tower of **Coleby Grange Airfield** soon comes into sight, but this short-lived airfield never had a paved runway and this site is now arable farmland, on which you are requested not to trespass. Driving east from the Boundary Cafe crossroads, you pass through Metheringham village and past the remains of **RAF Metheringham**, long since dismantled. Nearby is **Scopwick**, last resting place of several British, American, Canadian and, indeed, German airmen. At **Digby** and **Anwick** are the remains of two more airfields, the former having been the first to be bombed by the German Luftwaffe.

You now come to **Coningsby**, where you can enjoy a tour of the **Battle of Britain Memorial Flight's vintage aircraft**. See the chapter 'The RAF in Lincolnshire.' Eight miles (13 kms) further towards the coast near the A155 is **East Kirkby**, home of the **Lincolnshire Aviation Heritage Centre**, also featured in more detail in that chapter.

Retracing part of your route, you now proceed along the A153 to **Cranwell**, from which Britain's first ever jet plane, the Gloster E28/39, popularly known as the Pioneer or Whittle, first flew. Cranwell remains the **RAF's Flying Training School**. Passing **Leadenham**, once a sizeable aerodrome, you now head briefly north on the A607 for **RAF Wellingore**. Doubling back, you now take the A17 for Newark, heading towards the **Newark Air Museum**, north east of the town off the A46 at Winthorpe. Returning on the A46 to Lincoln, **Swinderby** is the last airfield passed on this part of the route.

One further detour is possible north to **RAF Scampton**, home of 617 Squadron (the 'Dam Busters') and the famous Red Arrows, and Hemswell, where there are some interesting aircraft exhibits at **Hemswell Antiques**.

Drive Five - for Animal Lovers

Route: Great Grimsby, Louth, Alford, Candlesby, Great Steeping, Burgh le Marsh, Skegness, Mablethorpe, Cleethorpes, Great Grimsby

Distance: 89 miles - 143 kms

Access: The two best points at which to join this route are Great Grimsby or Skegness.

General Description: This route enables the visitor to take in a number of the places mentioned in our feature 'Attractions for Animal Lovers.' Please note, that one other, **Our Little Farm** at Plungar in Nottinghamshire, is well out of range of this route but should certainly be visited another time.

Route Instructions: After visiting the **National Fishing Heritage Centre** at Great Grimsby, you take the inland A16 to Louth and then fork left on the twisting A157 to Withern, where you take the B1373 through Woodthorpe (where the Woodthorpe Hall Holiday Park is found) and then the A1104 through Alford which, incidentally, is the base for the excellent **Lincolnshire and South Humberside Trust for Nature Conservation**. Leaving on the B1196 through Willoughby, you meet the A158 and turn right to Candlesby and immediately left to Great Steeping, where you will find the **Northcote Heavy Horse Centre**.

Now follow minor roads to Burgh le Marsh and the A158 to Skegness, home of **Natureland**. The return journey is simple, using the twisting A52 to Mablethorpe, home of the **Animal Gardens**, and then the A1031 Coast Road to Cleethorpes, where you can visit **Jungle World**, before returning to Great Grimsby.

The Viking Way

The **Viking Way** is a long distance footpath which stretches all the way from Oakham, almost on the shores of Rutland Water, between Stamford and Melton Mowbray, to the Humber Bridge.

Distance: It is 116 miles -186 kms long, but the most appealing stretches of the Walk are divided into the following shorter sections, and for each of these a descriptive leaflet is available:

Bigby to Walesby (15 miles - 24 kms). This goes through the attractive villages and open countryside of the Lincolnshire Wolds.

Walesby to Donington-on-Bain (12 miles - 19 kms) This section traverses some of the prettiest Wolds countryside, giving some of the best views in the region.

Donington-on-Bain to Woodhall Spa (13 miles - 15 kms) Along this stretch, a mixture of grassland, small woods and hedgerow trees present a distinctive landscape. Woodhall Spa is an attractive and interesting town, well worth a bit of exploration.

Woodhall Spa to Lincoln (15 miles - 24 kms) This pleasant walk through the Witham Valley leads right to the marvellously interesting City of Lincoln, historically one of the most rewarding places to visit in the whole of England.

Lincoln to Byard's Leap (15 miles - 24 kms) This stretch of the walk is interesting in that it follows the western edge of the limestone escarpment known as the Lincoln Cliff and then explores the gentle slopes of Lincoln Heath, a thoroughly scenic route.

Byard's Leap to Woolsthorpe (16 miles - 26 kms) This last stretch passes westwards across the limestone escarpment and drops down through Allington into the low land of the Witham Valley. Near Woolsthorpe the route follows the towpath of the Grantham Canal. Woolsthorpe, birthplace of Sir Isaac Newton, is another most interesting place to explore.

All local TICs will have information about these sections of the Viking Way, and there is also an official Viking Way booklet detailing the whole walk.

Walk One - A Section of the Viking Way

Route: Caistor, Nettleton, Normanby le Wold, Claxby, Walesby, Tealby

Distance: 7½ miles - 12 kms

Access: Caistor lies south west of Grimsby, on the A46 road which leads to Market Rasen.

General Description: This short section from Caistor to Tealby travels across some classic Wolds countryside, much of which lies within the Area of Outstanding Natural Beauty, and visits some exceptional villages on the way.

Route Instructions: Caistor is a small market town high in the Wolds with splendid views, on a clear day, of Lincoln Cathedral. It is mentioned in the records of the Venerable Bede as being where the King of Wessex beat the King of Mercia in a great battle in 828 AD. But Caistor was here long before that, being not only the site of a Roman fort, as parts of the Roman Wall near the Church of St Peter and St Paul testify, but also of an ancient British Hill fort. The Church has traces of Anglo Saxon and Norman architecture, and the poet Sir Henry Newbolt attended the Grammar School.

Descend the path from the embankment on the A46 into Nettleton, which also has an ancient Church, and then follow the Nettleton Beck, entering the AONB. Evidence of mining for Claxby ironstone is still seen, and on the left of the path the red chalk is exposed in a quarry. You pass two abandoned medieval villages, Hardwick and Wykeham. Climbing to Acre House, join the road to Normanby le Wold, the highest settlement in the County. With Claxby Wood on your right, you now descend a grassy slope and cross a stream to enter Walesby (note all these '-by' endings, a sure sign of Viking origins).

Leaving Walesby past the Ramblers' Church, pass the farm at Risby, also once part of a medieval village, and descend past North Wold and Castle Farms to your final destination of Tealby, generally considered the Wolds' most lovely village. There is a fine Norman Church and the popular King's Head pub; but if you still have some energy left, do pursue the Way as far as Bayons Park before abandoning your walk. The manor house built by Tennyson's uncle, Charles Tennyson d'Eyncourt, in 1840, once stood here, embellished with every possible fortification, to make it look like a small castle.

THE VIKING WAY
(116 miles - 187 kms)

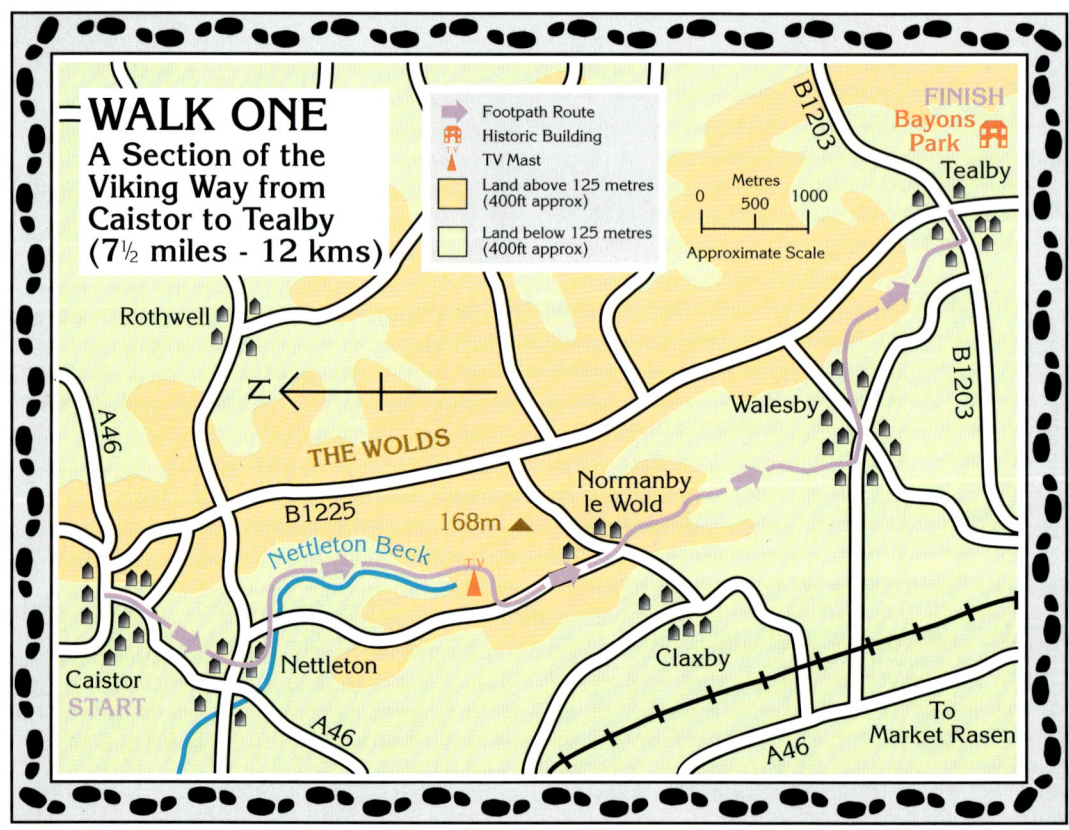

Legend:
- Footpath Route
- Tourist Information
- Historic Building
- Castle
- Art Gallery/Museum
- Cathedral
- Land above 125 metres (400ft approx)
- Land below 125 metres (400ft approx)

Approximate Scale: 0–16 Kms / 0–10 Miles

Locations: The Wash, River Humber, River Witham, THE WOLDS, Goulceby, Fulletby, Donington on Bain, Horncastle, Normanby le Wold, Tealby, Woodhall Spa, Caistor, Walesby, Barnety le Wold, Claxby, Nettleton, Bardney, Bigby, Wellingore, Byards Leap, FINISH Barton upon Humber, Lincoln, Waddington, Marston, Allington, START Oakham, Scunthorpe, Newark, Woolsthorpe, Woolsthorpe Manor

---

WALK ONE
A Section of the Viking Way from Caistor to Tealby
(7½ miles - 12 kms)

Legend:
- Footpath Route
- Historic Building
- TV Mast
- Land above 125 metres (400ft approx)
- Land below 125 metres (400ft approx)

Approximate Scale: 0–500–1000 Metres

Locations: FINISH Bayons Park, Tealby, B1203, Rothwell, Walesby, A46, THE WOLDS, Normanby le Wold, B1225, 168m, Nettleton Beck, T.V., Claxby, Caistor START, Nettleton, A46, To Market Rasen

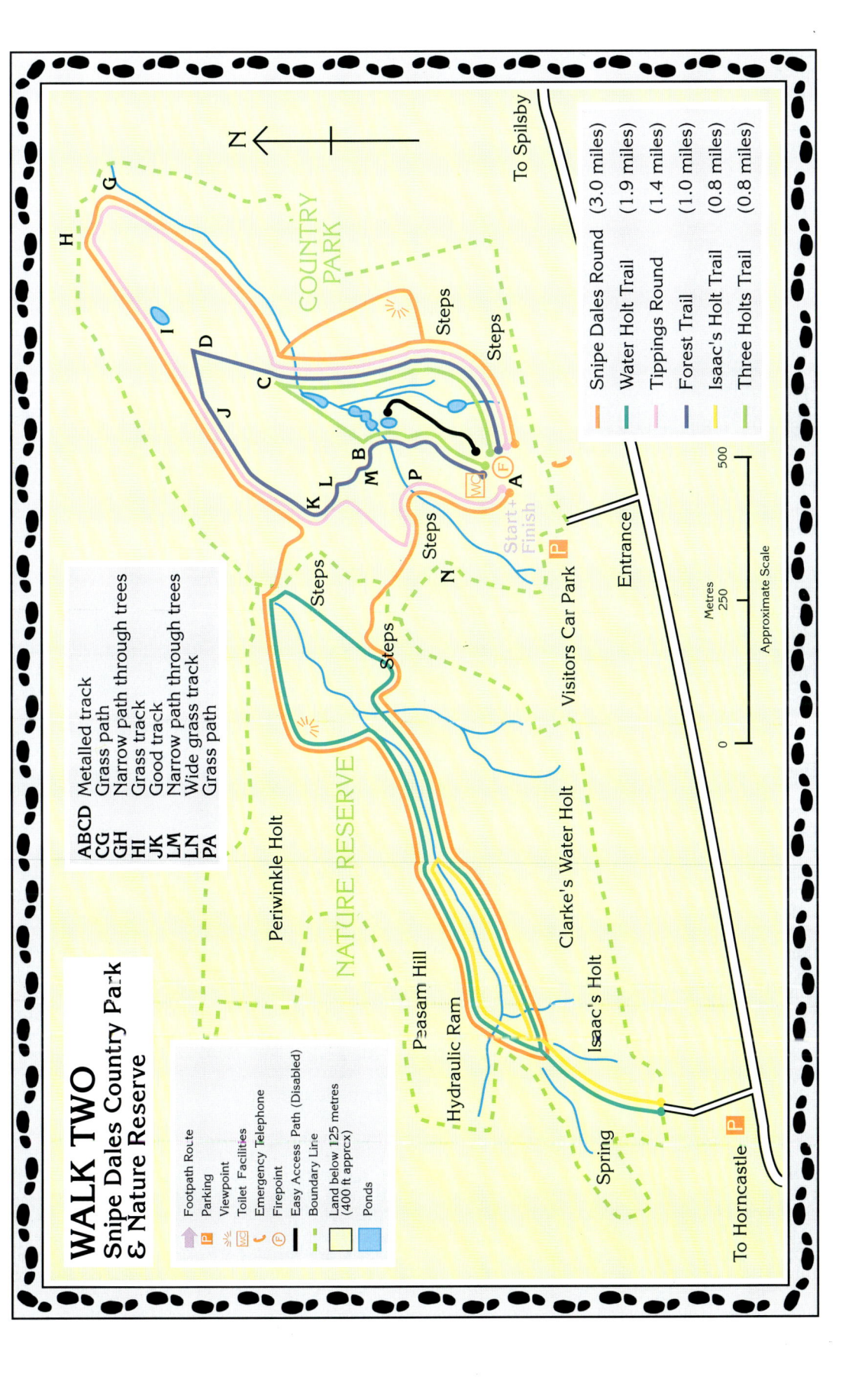

WALK TWO
Snipe Dales Country Park & Nature Reserve

ABCD Metalled track
CG Grass path
GH Narrow path through trees
HI Grass track
JK Good track
LM Narrow path through trees
LN Wide grass track
PA Grass path

Legend:
- Footpath Route
- Parking
- Viewpoint
- Toilet Facilities
- Emergency Telephone
- Firepoint
- Easy Access Path (Disabled)
- Boundary Line
- Land below 125 metres (400 ft approx)
- Ponds

Trails:
- Snipe Dales Round (3.0 miles)
- Water Holt Trail (1.9 miles)
- Tippings Round (1.4 miles)
- Forest Trail (1.0 miles)
- Isaac's Holt Trail (0.8 miles)
- Three Holts Trail (0.8 miles)

COUNTRY PARK
NATURE RESERVE

Periwinkle Holt
Peasam Hill
Hydraulic Ram
Clarke's Water Holt
Isaac's Holt
Spring

To Spilsby
To Horncastle

Visitors Car Park
Entrance
Start + Finish

Approximate Scale — Metres 0, 250, 500

N

Walk Two - Snipe Dales Country Park

Route: Six possible routes through the Snipe Dales Country Park and Nature Reserve, entitled Snipe Dales Round, Water Holt Trail, Tippings Round, Forest Trail, Isaac's Holt Trail and Three Holts Trail

Distance: The walks vary in length from slightly under a mile to 3 miles (nearly 5 kms), the length of the Snipe Dales Round.

Additional Walks: These are being added from September 1991 onwards. A 4 mile (6½ km) round walk to the village of Hagworthingham and back will be added in September 1991; and some 20 miles of footpaths are currently being developed into the wider countryside around Snipe Dales. These are being developed by the **Lincolnshire and South Humberside Trust for Nature Conservation,** in association with **Lincolnshire Recreational Services.**

Access: Snipe Dales lies to the north of the A1115, between Spilsby and Horncastle. There are two car parks, both clearly signposted, one giving entry to the more easterly **Country Park** and the other to the **Nature Reserve**.

Please note that a new section of path has now been added to the eastern side of the Country Park and this offers easy **access for the disabled** and an attractive viewpoint.

General Description: Snipe Dales is situated on the southern edge of the Wolds and consists of steep sided valleys fretted by streams, which have cut through the soft Spilsby sandstone into the Kimmeridge Clay below. At the junction of the sandstone and clay, there is a spring line giving rise to wet flushes and small streams. Wet valleys such as these were retained as woodland or managed as rough grazing, but in recent years much of this habitat has been converted to arable farming. Snipe Dales is one of the few substantial wet valley systems which still survive.

In the Country Park there are picturesque walks through some 36 hectares (90 acres) of mainly coniferous woodland, though many broad-leaved trees and shrubs have recently been introduced to give more diversity. Newly excavated ponds are being colonised by water plants and have attracted frogs, toads and dragonflies. There are picnic tables in pleasant surroundings by the car park, as well as by the central ponds and in a few other secluded areas.

The Nature Reserve consists of two main valleys, fretted by streams. The higher slopes are covered by rough grassland, whilst lower down at the junction of the sandstone and clay, the springline is indicated by tufted hair-grass rushes and ferns. A rich variety of flora is found in these differing habitats. Grazing by cattle and sheep has recently been resumed, with the aim of restoring a varied grass and herb community.

Route Instructions: There is not space here to describe in detail all of the six possible walks, so we focus on the **Water Holt Trail,** which visits the most interesting parts of the Nature Reserve. First, however, please note that there are three circular routes in the Country Park, two in the Nature Reserve (of which the Water Holt Trail is one) and the Snipe Dale Round, which links the two, forming a complete circuit of both Country Park and Nature Reserve.

The Water Holt Trail offers a scenic walk around the steep-sided main valley of the Nature Reserve, with many items of interest to see along the way. To follow the Trail (which is 1.9 miles long - approximately 3 kms), leave the Reserve Car Park and pass through the churchyard of the former St Mary's Church. Note the rookery in the sycamore and ash trees ahead. **Information boards** along the way tell you what birds and plants to look out for.

An old hydraulic ram thumps regularly in the valley bottom as it pumps water to the farm on the hill at Winceby. The footpath follows the stony bedded stream which is rich in invertebrates and where water voles may be seen. Eventually the path turns left up a hillside and there is the possibility of a short detour to a viewing point over the Wolds countryside. This is a good point from which to see the changing vegetation at the spring line. Barn owl and kestrel hunt regularly here and the green woodpecker may be heard.

Continue past a small plantation and gorse thicket to the main stream, where a path to the Country Park ascends the slope on the left. The main path passes through a wet area, which soon contrasts with a drier section of the route. Again, information boards are provided to help you identify the different plants which flourish in the two habitats. You can rejoin the entrance path at the footbridge.

Walk Three - The Peter Scott Walk

Route: West Lynn, alongside Great Ouse to Ongar Hill, across Terrington Marsh, to East Bank Picnic Place and parking on the bank of the River Nene

Distance: The entire walk is about 10 miles (16 kms) but it can be joined at any of three starting points (see below).

Access: There are three access points, West Lynn, to the west of King's Lynn on the south side of The Wash; Ongar Hill, which is signed from the A47 past Clenchwarton, then to Terrington Marsh and finally to Ongar Hill itself; and the East Bank Picnic Place near Sutton Bridge, which is a left turn off the A17 immediately you have crossed the River Nene.

General Description: The late **Sir Peter Scott**, well-known for his extreme love of coastal and wading birds, and founder of the **Wildfowl Trust** at Slimbridge in Gloucestershire (from which several other Trust Reserves have now developed), frequently came here, to the banks of The Wash and enjoyed watching the many birds. This walk, named in his honour, explores one of the few remaining areas of true fenland in Lincolnshire and offers an opportunity for the visitor to experience something of **the rich wildlife of the Fens,** which always delighted Sir Peter so much.

Route Instructions: Starting from the West Lynn entry point, the walk at first follows the left bank of the River Great Ouse. It hardly seems like a river bank, of course, because all this land has been reclaimed from the sea from what was once a vast, spreading estuary. Occupying a man-made channel, therefore, the River runs dead straight towards the sea.

When the thaw finally came after the last Ice Age, the waters of The Wash spread inland for several miles, as far as Mildenhall. Between land and sea lay a wide, marshy area, made up of coastal silts and muds, with the richer peaty soils stretching inland.

Water-loving plants such as reeds and sedges were all that grew here, though wherever the land was a little higher (and consequently a little drier) scrubby woodland would have been present, comprised of oak, pine and yew and such shrubby undergrowth as bog myrtle. The richness of the underlying peat soils was hugely attractive to the earliest farmer, however, who knew that they could exploit this soil to grow better crops than almost anywhere else in England. **The Romans were the first to start draining the Fens,** cutting some massive dykes to carry the water away, such as the Car Dyke, which runs all the way from Lincoln to Cambridge. The immensity of this labour, in terms of man-hours, is almost too great to imagine, but perhaps it should not surprise us from the same people who were able to build Hadrian's Wall in Northumberland and the great roads, such as the Fosse and Ermine Ways, which traversed the entire country!

Throughout the Middle Ages, the sea level was actually slowly dropping, which put more and more of the Fenland within reach, so that by the C14th this had become by far **the most prosperous arable farming area in the whole of Britain.** There was some pasturage too, however, and the reed beds were cut for thatch, so almost all areas were effectively put to use.

A third phase of drainage was initiated in the C17th by the great Dutch engineer, **Vermuyden,** though in the area of The Wash this was not entirely successful, as the drainage scheme, based on the construction of the Old and New Bedford Rivers, ceased to function as the peat beds shrank back, deprived of water.

Even since then, however, more land has been reclaimed - indeed, as much as a mile has been added since Sir Peter Scott himself lived in the East Lighthouse in the 1930s. Our walk has not yet reached that point, however. First we have to cross the **Terrington Marshland**.

Saltmarsh muds and silts are especially attractive to **wading birds,** who find it populated by a whole host of small invertebrates. The birds you will see here are all ideally adapted to life in this habitat, walking on long thin legs and having long bills with which to probe around in the mud. They vary in size from birds as small as the ringed plover and little stint to the elegant curlew and the handsome black and white oyster catcher. Meanwhile, the sandbanks of the coast are the breeding grounds for the **largest colony of common seals in Europe.**

Incidentally, it is important to keep to the banks as the marshland can be dangerous. The walk ends where the two lighthouses face each other across the River Nene.

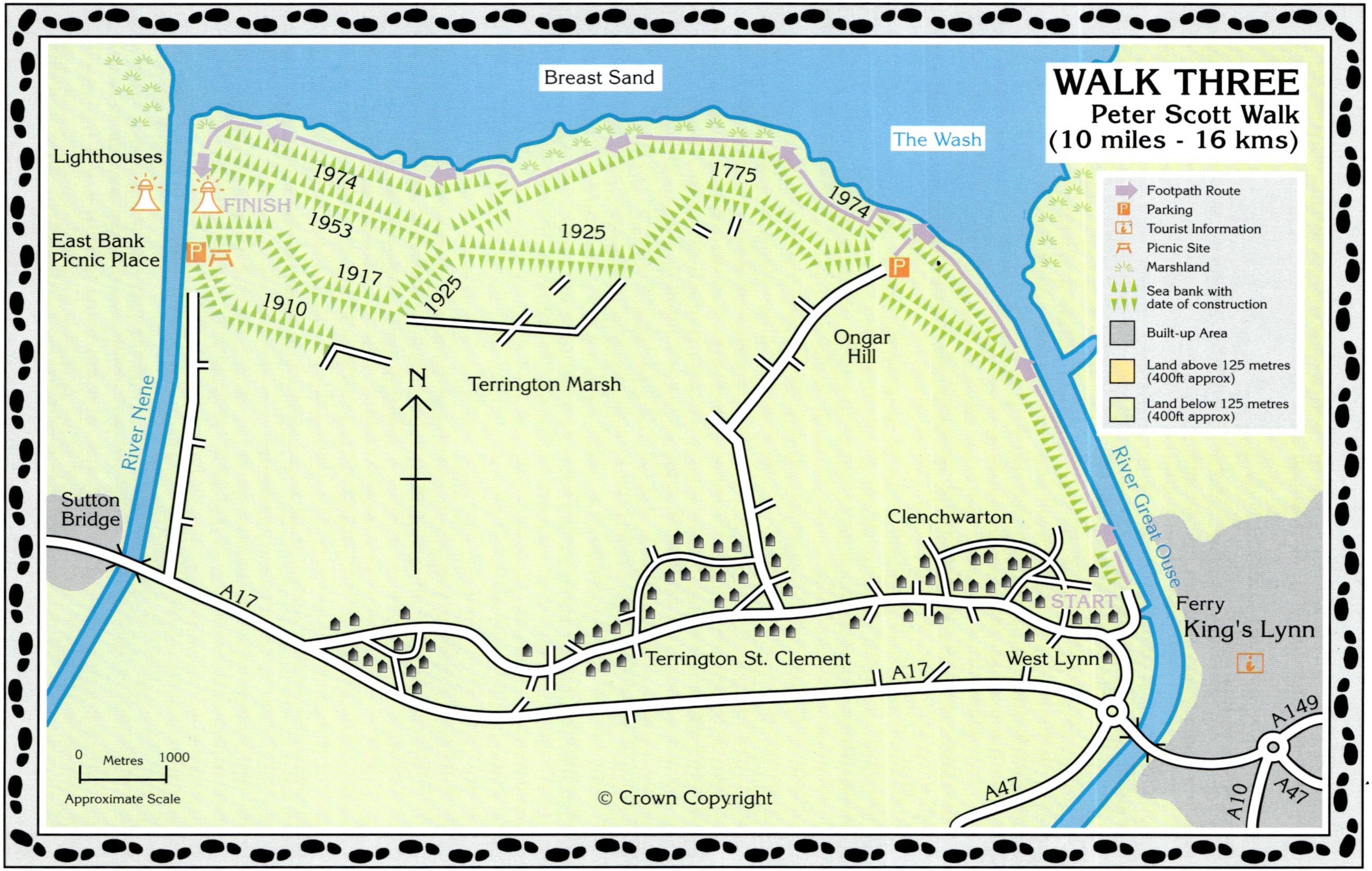
WALK THREE
Peter Scott Walk
(10 miles - 16 kms)
Footpath Route
Parking
Tourist Information
Picnic Site
Marshland
Sea bank with date of construction
Built-up Area
Land above 125 metres (400ft approx)
Land below 125 metres (400ft approx)
Breast Sand
The Wash
Lighthouses
FINISH
East Bank Picnic Place
1974
1953
1917
1910
1925
1925
1775
1974
N
Terrington Marsh
Ongar Hill
River Nene
Sutton Bridge
A17
Clenchwarton
START
Terrington St. Clement
A17
West Lynn
River Great Ouse
Ferry
King's Lynn
A149
A47
A10
A47
0 Metres 1000
Approximate Scale
© Crown Copyright

WALK FOUR
River Slea Trail
(8 miles - 13 kms)

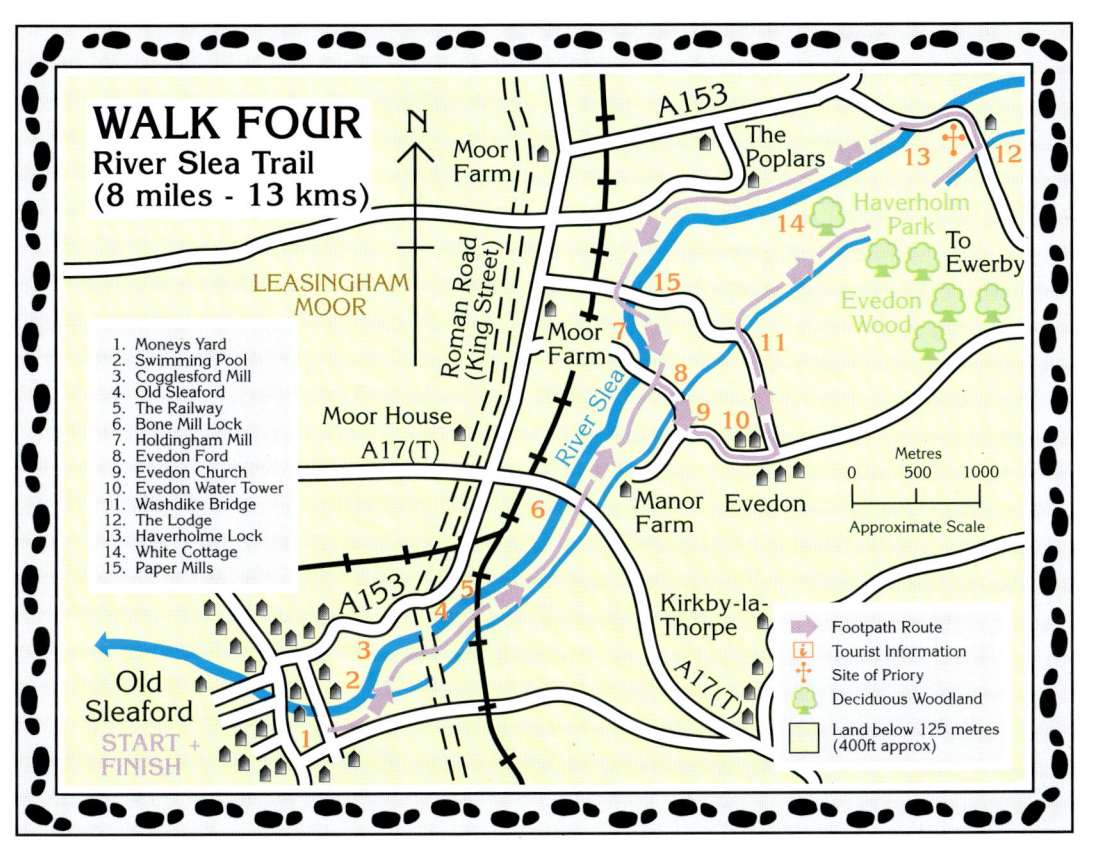

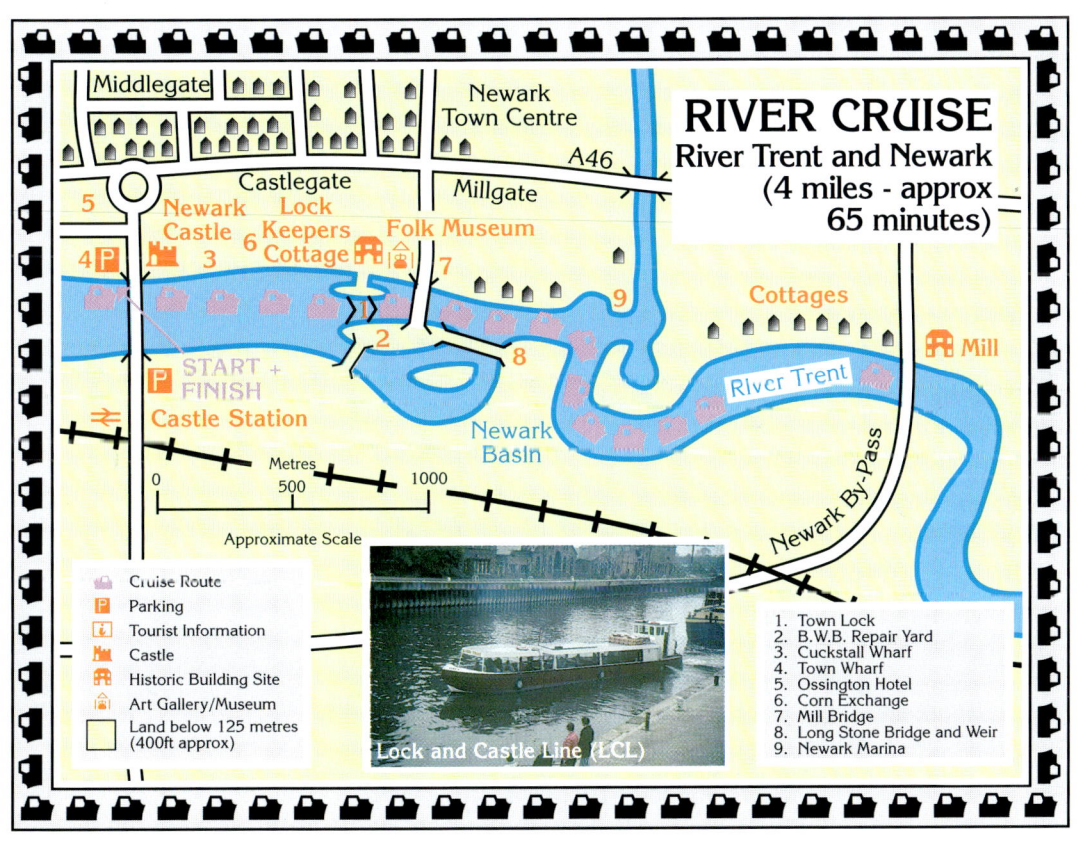

1. Moneys Yard
2. Swimming Pool
3. Cogglesford Mill
4. Old Sleaford
5. The Railway
6. Bone Mill Lock
7. Holdingham Mill
8. Evedon Ford
9. Evedon Church
10. Evedon Water Tower
11. Washdike Bridge
12. The Lodge
13. Haverholme Lock
14. White Cottage
15. Paper Mills

N

A153
Moor Farm
The Poplars
Haverholm Park
To Ewerby
Evedon Wood
LEASINGHAM MOOR
Roman Road (King Street)
Moor Farm
River Slea
Moor House
A17(T)
Manor Farm
Evedon
Kirkby-la-Thorpe
A17(T)
A153
Old Sleaford
START + FINISH

Metres 0 500 1000
Approximate Scale

- Footpath Route
- Tourist Information
- Site of Priory
- Deciduous Woodland
- Land below 125 metres (400ft approx)

RIVER CRUISE
River Trent and Newark
(4 miles - approx 65 minutes)

Middlegate
Newark Town Centre
A46
Castlegate
Millgate
Newark Castle
Lock Keepers Cottage
Folk Museum
START + FINISH
Castle Station
Newark Basin
Cottages
Mill
River Trent
Newark By-Pass

Metres 0 500 1000
Approximate Scale

- Cruise Route
- Parking
- Tourist Information
- Castle
- Historic Building Site
- Art Gallery/Museum
- Land below 125 metres (400ft approx)

1. Town Lock
2. B.W.B. Repair Yard
3. Cuckstall Wharf
4. Town Wharf
5. Ossington Hotel
6. Corn Exchange
7. Mill Bridge
8. Long Stone Bridge and Weir
9. Newark Marina

Lock and Castle Line (LCL)

Walk Four - The River Slea Trail

Route: The Trail follows the River Slea Navigation from Sleaford to Haverholme

Distance: About 8 miles - 13 kms

Route Instructions: Leave Money's Yard, where the old windmill, now sail-less, is used as a TIC, via Berkeley Court; take the paved path past the Civic Trust's water garden and Sleaford Swimming Pool, and follow the New Slea to the bridge. **Cogglesford Mill**, an old grain mill, is near the first of the seven locks. Keeping to the riverside, with Cogglesford on your left, go through the gate at the end of the woods. In this area of really ancient settlement, Stone Age, Iron Age, Roman and Anglo Saxon remains have all been found. Continue to a monument to a much later age, the railway bridge - and reflect that it was the coming of the railways that effectively killed the canals. Take a tunnel under the line and continue to the next bridge. **Bone Mill Lock** was where old animal bones were crushed to make fertiliser. Follow the path under the bridge to the next lock and **Holdingham Mill**, where there is an octagonal tollbooth. A footbridge crosses the Slea at **Evedon Ford** and continues to **Evedon Church**, which dates from the C13th but has been much altered since. The water tower, now a private house, is typical of its kind.

Follow the road into the village, keeping left at both junctions, to the **Washdike Bridge**. The path now goes through Evedon Wood past Haverholme Park, now demolished. At the paved road, turn left to the old **Haverholme Lock**, which you cross to turn left onto the riverside path. Pass White Cottage with its pretty (private) garden and cross over the bridge to your left. Pass the remains of **Evedon Paper Mill** and, keeping the river on your right, return to **Sleaford**.

River Cruise in Newark

Upon leaving **Town Wharf**, overlooked by the imposing Ossington Hotel, and starting upstream towards Bottingham, on this 65 minute trip, you straight away realise this is a voyage of discovery. Gliding peacefully under the C18th bridge, you can clearly see the footpaths which were added to the bridge in 1848 to convey pedestrians safely past horses and carriages to the newly built railway station. Passing under the bridge, look left and catch a glimpse of the **Toll House** dwarfed by **Newark Castle**.

Newark Castle, built in 1129 by the Bishop of Lincoln, was where a very ill **King John**, of Magna Carta fame, died in 1216. Charles I's forces finally surrendered there at the end of the Civil War in 1646, after which much of the building was demolished. The wharf adjacent to the Castle was known as **Cuckstall Wharf**. In medieval times 'nagging wives' were brought to this spot for a ducking in the 'cuckstall'. The building on the hill is the **Corn Exchange**, designed by Sir Henry Dewsbury and completed in 1847. Facing the town with its back to the river, its frontage has the architectural grandeur of a small town hall.

As you approach **Town Lock** notice, on the left, the entrance to the old lock built in 1773. On the right, the weir stream joins the main river. After rising two metres in the lock, you can see the original lock keeper's cottage, built in 1779. You now enter **Newark Basin**, a C19th hive of activity, where tastefully converted warehouses have been utilised as workshops, houses, a Brasserie and **Folk Museum**. A cobbled riverside walk winds its way through these buildings to **Mill Bridge**. On the opposite bank is British Waterways busy repair yard. Just like the traditional canal painting of a bridge with countryside beyond, so Mill Bridge crystallises the transition from town to country. On the left are some very attractive new private houses whose owners produce flowers in profusion from every balcony, wall and crevice. On the right is **Long Stone Bridge** which carried the original towpath across the weir stream and out into the country.

Peaceful, rural Nottinghamshire: Relax, breathe in the quiet and soak up the tranquillity. Look into the distance and see a little group of houses, built along the river bank by the mill owner, whose derelict mill stands as a sentinel to times past. Neatly and unobtrusively slipped in between mill and houses glistens the new Newark By-Pass, a great help to the town and a very commendable piece of modern architecture. By-Pass, mill and reed beds viewed at close quarters, it is now time to start the return journey - along which, remember to keep a keen eye open for herons, kingfishers clapper-gates, roving stones and even the remains of a World War II fuel storage wharf.

Selected Museums to Visit

These pages look at a number of selected Museums. Please note that several others are listed in the chapter on the RAF in Lincolnshire and there is a complete list in the Directory section at the back of the guide.

THE BOSTON GUILDHALL MUSEUM occupies a fine brick structure dating back to 1450, once the Hall of the St Mary's Guild and later the Town Hall for the Corporation of Boston. In the Museum, **the original prison cells** in which the religious separatists, later known as the **'Pilgrim Fathers'** were imprisoned in 1607, are on view. There is also an ancient kitchen, equipped as in the early C17th. **The Maritime Room** houses an interesting display of ship models and custom house artefacts. The Council Chamber retains a C15th deed cupboard with linenfold carved doors. **The Courtroom** witnessed the most noteworthy trial of the 'Pilgrim Fathers' in September 1607. **The Banqueting Hall** has a Musicians' Balcony and a stone-mullioned west window with ancient stained glass. Exhibits include displays on archaeology, costume and textiles, ceramics, militaria, coins, fine art and agriculture, reflecting the local history of the Borough.

A wide variety of monthly exhibitions is seen in the entrance hall all year. There is also a shop selling a wide range of booklets, postcards and souvenir items. The Boston Guildhall Museum is open Mondays-Saturdays 10am-5pm all year. Sundays 1.30-5pm April to end of September. Closed at Christmas and New Year Bank Holidays. The admission charge includes use of a personal audio guided tour. For further details contact Boston Guildhall Museum, South Street, Boston, Lincolnshire PE21 6HT. Telephone (0205) 365954.

RUTLAND COTTAGE MUSIC AND FAIRGROUND MUSEUM is a fascinating collection of Mechanical Musical Instruments and Fairground Bygones. It has been featured on BBC, Anglia and Yorkshire TV and broadcasts have been made from the museum on BBC and Commercial Radio many times.

Visitors are taken on a conducted tour and the history and development of mechanical entertainment is demonstrated by the playing of various instruments. You are taken back in time to the early 1800s when you listen to **Music-Boxes**, the first means of home entertainment. Their development is traced when you listen to Disc Music Boxes, Barrel Organs, Edison Phonographs, Player Pianos and many more. Also there are early pianos, Reed Organs, Church Pipe Organs, and Cinema Organs. The Museum houses a **unique collection of over 12,000 Gramophone Records,** dating from 1900 to the present time, and a fascinating collection of Circus Posters covering the last 100 years of Circus. It is also the home of **Tillers Royal Marionettes**, which travelled the fairs in England as long ago as 1790, and the famous 'Lilliput Theatre', which toured America as the smallest theatre in the World.

In the grounds of the Museum is a small **Edwardian Fair** of the 1920s era, complete with Portable Theatre, with performances by the **Zodiac Living Marionettes** every weekend from May. Children of all ages can sample the delights of a real Old Tyme Fair.

THE VINA COOKE MUSEUM is just over the border from Lincolnshire, but easily accessible from Lincoln, Sleaford or Grantham, in the village of Cromwell. Here you will find a remarkable collection of **Dolls and all kinds of Childhood Bygones,** loved by young and old alike.

Four miles (6 kms) north of Newark on the A1, turn into Cromwell and up the drive by the churchyard wall. **The fine C17th house**, a former rectory, has links with the Cromwell family (Ralph, Lord Cromwell of Tattershall amongst them); also with the Earls of Lincoln, as several generations of Fiennes-Clintons, members of that illustrious family, lived here as Rectors. Many of their children were born and grew up here, and you may catch their echoes as you wander through the rooms now occupied by the magical collection of dolls, toys and costumes which make up this fascinating museum. Incidentally, their Nanny still haunts the rooms, so you may feel you are being scrutinised.

Handmade dolls in porcelain and cloth are made on the premises, and are for sale. Home-prepared refreshments are available in the splendid tearoom, or a grassy picnic area in the garden. **Home-grown plants and herbs** may be purchased. You will savour a personal welcome to this unique attraction. Every Easter Monday a special event takes place, with an open-air accent - Morris Dancers, Craft Stalls, Working Models, Handbell-Ringers and many other entertainments make this a special festival for the Museum and its visitors.

STAMFORD STEAM BREWERY MUSEUM

The museum is located in the centre of Stamford. Car parks located in Scotgate and Sheepmarket are 5 minutes' walk away. The Station Road bus park for coaches is also nearby.

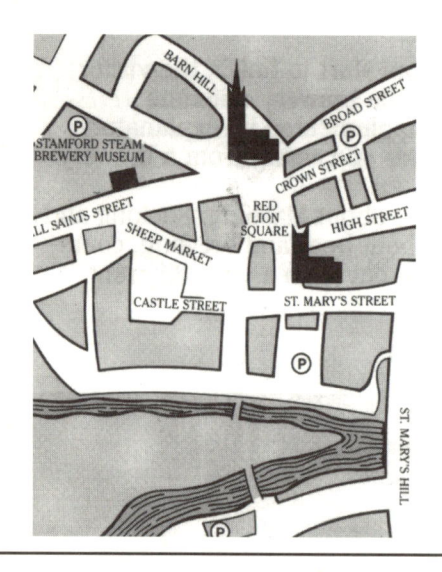

Complete Victorian Steam Brewery

The museum is open from: Wednesday – Sunday (inclusive) 1st April – 30th September 10am – 4pm
Open Bank Holidays April – September 10am – 4 pm Closed Wednesdays during Bank Holiday weeks.
Evening Parties by arrangement.

Tel: (0780) 52186.

**For further information please write to:–
Stamford Steam Brewery Museum
All Saints Street
Stamford, Lincs. PE9 2PA.**

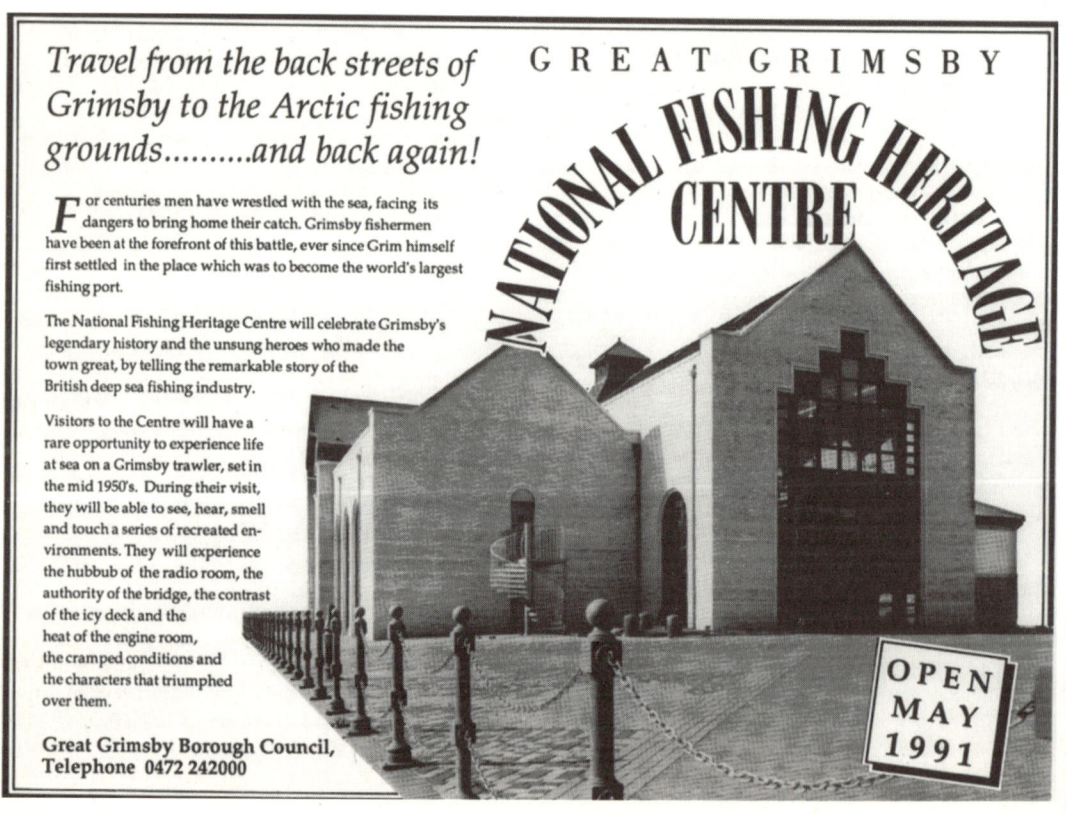

GREAT GRIMSBY NATIONAL FISHING HERITAGE CENTRE

Travel from the back streets of Grimsby to the Arctic fishing grounds..........and back again!

For centuries men have wrestled with the sea, facing its dangers to bring home their catch. Grimsby fishermen have been at the forefront of this battle, ever since Grim himself first settled in the place which was to become the world's largest fishing port.

The National Fishing Heritage Centre will celebrate Grimsby's legendary history and the unsung heroes who made the town great, by telling the remarkable story of the British deep sea fishing industry.

Visitors to the Centre will have a rare opportunity to experience life at sea on a Grimsby trawler, set in the mid 1950's. During their visit, they will be able to see, hear, smell and touch a series of recreated environments. They will experience the hubbub of the radio room, the authority of the bridge, the contrast of the icy deck and the heat of the engine room, the cramped conditions and the characters that triumphed over them.

**Great Grimsby Borough Council,
Telephone 0472 242000**

OPEN MAY 1991

Steam Brewery Museum, Stamford

This Museum is a complete **Victorian Steam Brewery**. It was founded in 1825 by William Brown Edwards, and then taken over by Herbert Wells Melbourn in 1869. The Brewery produced Melbourn's Ales for over a hundred years until production ceased in July 1974. When the Brewery opened as a Museum in 1978, it still contained all the original equipment, including a mash tun, coppers, fermenting vessels and a steam engine, which was built by Marshall and Sons of Gainsborough in 1910.

Visitors can follow **the brewing process** from start to finish and will learn the meaning of terms such as mashing, sparging, and racking. An automatic sound system describes the function of each room and, together with the reminiscences of one of the Brewery's lifetime workers, visitors are given an insight into the working conditions of a C19th brewery employee.

The Brewery is set amidst attractive stone buildings, with timbered roofs covered in collyweston slating. Although the brew house dates back to Victorian times, parts of the buildings are believed to be much older, probably Tudor, while the street frontage is Regency. The Museum features displays of **Victorian working life**, including a Head Brewer's office, laboratory and cooperage. Corking machines and a 'Boot and Flogger' are also to be seen, and there is a collection of drinking jars and advertising material of the period with, by way of a contrast, a display of more recent packaging.

The Museum is open between the 1st April and the 30th September, Wednesday-Sunday inclusive. It is open Bank Holiday Mondays but is closed on Wednesdays during these weeks. Opening hours are 10am-4pm. **Evening visits** can be arranged in advance, when, after a tour of the Brewery, the Museum Bar is open for refreshments.

The Museum is in the centre of Stamford, with car parking facilities nearby in Scotgate and Sheepmarket, and the bus station only two minutes walk away. So, if you would like to see how real ale was made in the C19th, come along to the Stamford Steam Brewery Museum for an experience with a very different flavour.

National Fishing Heritage Centre

Visitors to the **National Fishing Heritage Centre** at Grimsby sign on as crew members of a 1950s steam trawler and journey to the Arctic fishing grounds. You can handle the trawler controls, feel the pitch and roll of the ship, hear the cries of the fishermen pulling in bursting nets, suffer the pungent smells, and endure the heat and noise of the engine room. Moreover, an ingenious cooling system and wind machine allow you to experience Arctic conditions, while computers bring the ship's equipment to life and videos help to complete the sensation of being on board.

The exhibition evokes every possible aspect of the trade from finding the fish to landing the catch. Visitors will encounter the hubbub of the radio room, the authority of the bridge and the bustle of the dock, as the lumpers unload the fish. In fact, this themed attraction, using genuine parts of old trawlers, a ship's galley and fo'c'sle among them, is based on real people and historical facts.

The National Fishing Heritage Centre also contains a large **internal dock**, where the Perseverance fishing smack floats fully rigged and under sail. She is a Boston shrimper and was the last all-sail fishing vessel to operate from Great Grimsby fish docks. In addition, there are four prestigious galleries, used for a **changing programme of exhibitions** devoted to all aspects of Industrial fishing addressing local, national and international topics.

The National Fishing Heritage Centre is the lynch pin of an ambitious scheme to redevelop the **Alexandra Dock.** By the end of 1992, the 6 hectare (15 acre) site will include an 85 bedroom Ibis hotel, shops, water sports centre, theme pub, fish restaurant, museum and craft workshops, all carefully designed to give visitors an impression of Great Grimsby in the C19th. A restored paddle steamer, the Lincoln Castle, already provides a carvery, lounge bar and conference facility.

Traffic-free urban squares, connected by pedestrian pathways, will become the focus for a free entertainments programme, **'Down at the Docks'**, which will involve a host of street performers. A themed 1950s nautical school room can be booked by schools and adult education groups. A variety of materials will be available including handling collections, working models, and videos.

Step back in time and visit the
GUILDHALL MUSEUM

See the original cells and courtroom where the
PILGRIM FATHERS
were imprisoned and tried in 1607 Pictures and prints of local interest, customs artefacts, archaeological, material, ancient fire marks and maritime room OPEN MONDAY TO SATURDAY, 10am - 5pm throughout the year. Also Sunday 1.30pm – 5pm April to September Admission charge includes use of personal audio guided tour

FREE ADMISSION FOR CHILDREN

SOUTH STREET, BOSTON
Tel. (0205) 365954

The Red Lion Hotel

RECENTLY REFURBISHED
18th CENTURY HOTEL

ENSUITE ACCOMMODATION

REAL ALES - REAL FOOD

WARM WELCOME & VALUE
FOR MONEY

Market Place, Spalding, Lincs. PE11 1SU.
Tel: (0775) 722869

THE VINA COOKE
MUSEUM OF DOLLS & BYGONE CHILDHOOD

Large collection of Victorian dolls, toys, prams, doll's houses, books, trains, christening robes, costumes and hand-made character dolls of Vina Cooke
All this and more in a grand 17th century house next to the church in the village of Cromwell, 4 miles north of Newark on the A1 CAR AND COACH PARKING FREE
Home-prepared refreshments available (booking advisable)
Admission: £1 Adults, 50p Children
Bus parties, WI and school parties catered for **Open any time during the day and evening** (by appointment in evening)
Telephone 0636 821 364
The Old Rectory Cromwell, Newark, Notts NG23 6JE

Rutland Cottage

MECHANICAL MUSIC & FAIRGROUND MUSEUM

Come and take a Nostalgic Trip into the Past with Mechanical Music, Organs, Marionettes and the original Lilliput Theatre.
A DAY OUT FOR ALL

Picnic Area Amusements
Childrens Play Area All Set in
5 acres of grounds.
MILLGATE
WHAPLODE ST. CATHERINES
NR. SPALDING LINCOLNSHIRE
Tel 040 634 379

Opening times:- Saturdays, Sundays & Bank Holidays: 10am to 6pm. From Easter to end of September. July, August & September: 2pm to 5pm, Monday to Friday. Other times by appointment

Museums in the City of Lincoln

There are three museums in Lincoln itself, which, between them, give an over-view of **the richness and variety of the County's heritage.**

THE USHER GALLERY in Danesgate was built in 1927, to house a wonderful collection of watches, miniatures and porcelain bequeathed to the city by local jeweller James Ward Usher, who made his fortune by popularising the **Lincoln Imp**. He was a jeweller by profession and his bequest to the City resulted in the building of this remarkable gallery, erected in 1927 and set in lovely grounds.

Now in addition to the Usher Collection, the Gallery has paintings, clocks, coins and medals, furniture, and memorabilia relating to **Alfred Tennyson**, the Victorian Poet Laureate. These last include his coat and hat, among other personal possessions.

A visit to the collection of coins, already mentioned, is imperative if you are a keen numismatist, as there are superb displays of coins reaching right back to Roman times. They include the Sir Francis Hill collection of Lincolnshire coins and tokens.

There are a number of **portraits of Lincolnshire people,** including a magnificent picture of Sir Joseph Banks, the famous botanist who, with Captain Cook, discovered Botany Bay and is known as the Father of Australia.

The collection of **watercolours by Peter de Wint**, a near contemporary of Turner and Constable, is the largest in the country and contains many local scenes. Despite his Dutch-sounding name, de Wint was an Englishman who spent much of his life in Lincolnshire, the county from which his wife came.

Amongst the **clocks** are two extremely rare examples of all-wooden movements constructed by Robert Sutton of Barton on Humber. Other features include an exhibition gallery, named after Miss Ella Curtois of Branston, whose **sculptures** are on display along with work by other artists.

There is also a fine collection of Torskey and Pinxton **porcelain** on loan from the Exley family, and a good collection of paintings provided by the Heslam Memorial Trust, set up in memory of John Heslam of Scunthorpe in 1963. **C20th paintings** include works by L.S.Lowry and John Piper. The Gallery also has an interesting and innovative **temporary exhibition programme,** as well as **workshops,** a marvellous sequence of lunch-time and other **concerts and other events** - it is in fact a real treasure house.

THE CITY AND COUNTY MUSEUM is itself housed inside a major exhibit - **a C13th building** which was once used by the Greyfriars and has very impressive stone vaulting on the ground floor.

The Museum houses the County's **archaeology and natural history collections.** Lincoln was a major Roman town and some idea of the impression made on the local population by the coming of the legions can be gained from the model of the 9th Legion approaching Lincoln with its total complement of 5,500 men.

The Museum is also currently home to Lincoln Cathedral's exemplar of **Magna Carta** - the original document which laid the foundation for our current democratic society as long ago as 1215.

If you are researching your family history with Lincolnshire connections or you want to know more about Lincolnshire people and places, then plan a visit to the **Lincolnshire Archives,** a treasure house of the past.

THE MUSEUM OF LINCOLNSHIRE LIFE in Burton Road brings the story of the County up to the present day. This large and popular Museum is crammed full of fascinating items from tanks to teddy bears and from socks to steam engines (the first tank was in fact designed and built in Lincoln).

Domestic, community and commercial life are covered together with crafts, trades and industries and, of course, agriculture - the most important aspect of the County's history. The drainage of the fens and the Agricultural Revolution are covered, and farm machinery old and new is on display, much of it made by the great engineering firms of Lincolnshire, like Robeys and Rustons.

The Museum also houses the collection of the **Royal Lincolnshire Regiment and of the Lincolnshire Yeomanry,** for whom the present museum buildings - the Old Barracks - were constructed in 1857.

Grimsthorpe Castle

LINCOLNSHIRE
(A151 Colsterworth to Bourne Road.)

A Stately Home in the occupation of the Barons Willoughby de Eresby since 1516. Architecture comprises a Medieval tower. Tudor quadrangular house with a Vanbrugh North front and Neo-Gothic west front. Public Tours - 8 State Rooms and 2 Picture Galleries with an important collection of furniture, pictures and tapestries, porcelain etc. Gardens and Park a special feature.

<u>1991</u>
Gardens and Park. Open Saturdays, Sundays & Bank Holidays 4th May to 15th September. 10am to 6pm. Adults £1 O.A.Ps & under 16yrs. 50p. Castle. Open Sundays and Bank Holidays. 26th May to 15th September. 2pm to 6pm (No admission after 5.30pm,) Adults £2 O.A.Ps, Students & under 16yrs. £1 Home made teas available in the Coach House. Tea Rooms.

Conducted Tours for Private Parties (May to September) by arrangement with the Trust Manager,
The Estate Office, Grimsthorpe,
Bourne, Lincs. PE10 0NB

Rob and Sue welcome you to

The Ship Inn

Morning Coffee
Bar Snacks
Evening Meals
Sunday Lunches
Beer Garden
Children Welcome

**Northgate, Pinchbeck.
Telephone 723792**

MAKE YOUR VISIT COMPLETE WITH OUR HERITAGE SERIES OF PUBLICATIONS

TITLES INCLUDE:
Weardale, Barnard Castle and Upper Teesdale, Middleton-in-Teesdale, Eden Valley, Swaledale, Wensleydale, Herriot Country, Captain James Cook, Malham & Airedale, Wharfedale and Summer Wine Country

WIDELY AVAILABLE THROUGHOUT THE COUNTRY OR BY MAIL ORDER FROM:

Discovery Guides Ltd.
1 Market Place, Middleton-in-Teesdale, Co Durham DL12 0QG.
Telephone 0833 40638

THE BEST OF BRITAIN

Selected Historic Buildings

It is not possible here to detail all the multitude of historic buildings which claim the attention in Lincolnshire - for that you must turn to the Directory pages at the back of the book. Here, we focus on a few selected places we hope visitors will enjoy.

GAINSBOROUGH OLD HALL is a perfectly preserved medieval manor house set in the middle of the small market town of Gainsborough. The timber-framed house was built on a grand scale by **Sir Thomas Burgh** between 1460 and the 1480s. The magnificent **Great Hall**, with its spectacular high arched roof, forms the centre of the house. **The original Kitchens** survive and they are set out to portray the busy day in 1483 when King Richard III stayed at the Old Hall, and cooks and scullions prepared mounds of food for a feast. Two wings and a brick Tower complete the building.

The Old Hall has later connections with the **Mayflower Pilgrims**, many of whom originated in this part of England. Two room settings of 1607, when they worshipped in the Old Hall, and a permanent exhibition, mark this episode in the building's exciting history. Other exhibitions tell the story of the building itself, and its connections with Richard III and Henry VIII.

Visitors can enjoy the Old Hall's quiet atmosphere with the help of a free Soundalive taped guide, or they can attend the **regular special events** that bring the building to life throughout the year, such as the May Fair and several Craft Fairs. The Year's highlight is the Living History Weekend, when the house returns to two days 300 or 400 years ago, and is populated with the household of the time, complete with farm animals in the yard.

The Shop and Tea Shop are open daily. Other catering and guided tours can be arranged. The education programme has won a Sandford Award and there is an active Friends Association. Gainsborough Old Hall, owned by English Heritage and managed by Lincolnshire County Council, is open Monday-Saturday, 10am-5pm and on Sundays from Easter to October 31st, 2-5pm.

GRIMSTHORPE CASTLE is the home of the **Willoughby de Eresby** family created Barons in 1313. It was given to the Willoughby de Eresbys in 1516 as a wedding present by Henry VIII, when the 10th Lord Willoughby de Eresby married Maria de Salinas, a cousin of Henry VIII's wife, Katherine of Aragon. The oldest part of the Castle is a medieval Tower built in the early part of the C13th, probably by Gilbert de Gant, Earl of Lincoln. In 1542, to accommodate a **Royal Visit by Henry VIII**, the Duke of Suffolk, husband of the Baroness Willoughby de Eresby, extended the Castle, forming a quadrangle house around an inner courtyard incorporating the original medieval tower.

In 1715 the 16th Lord Willoughby de Eresby was created Duke of Ancaster, who employed **Sir John Vanbrugh** to rebuild the castle in a more opulent style. Only the North front was completed. Vanbrugh died before the work was finished, Grimsthorpe being Vanbrugh's last work. In the early part of the C19th, the West front was rebuilt in the neo-Gothic style by the architect Henry Garling. Visitors to Grimsthorpe are consequently able to see four different periods of architecture.

The formal gardens are the work over the years of **Capability Brown** and **Stephen Switzer**. The parkland in front of the castle was probably designed by Capability Brown, but the 40 acre lake was the work of the Spalding engineer and surveyor, John Grundy. In 1956 the fruit and vegetable gardens were laid out by the late Lady Ancaster and Peter Coats. In July and August **Nature Trails** are routed through the park by the Lincolnshire and South Humberside Trust for Nature Conservation. There is ample parking for cars and coaches, a picnic area with views of the castle and lake, and a Tea Room with facilities for the disabled.

DODDINGTON HALL The splendid outline of a magnificent Elizabethan mansion comes as a surprise in the flat Lincolnshire countryside. Doddington Hall, completed in 1600 by Robert Smythson, survives unaltered today with its Gatehouse and courtyards as one of the most beautiful houses of its period in the country.

The Hall is built of mellow pink brick and honey coloured stone, and it stands in 2 hectares (5 acres) of sheltered walled gardens, surrounded by an unspoilt village. Within, four centuries of continuous occupation, by four families in turn, have left a rich inheritance of china, pictures, tapestries and furniture, set in simple **Georgian interiors** and lit by huge windows. The house is blessed with its own uniquely friendly atmosphere, and the visitor passes through a succession of elegant and spacious

DODDINGTON HALL and GARDENS

A beautiful Elizabethan Mansion set in five acres of romantic walled gardens. Only a few minutes drive from central Lincoln, and one of the finest houses of the Age in the whole Country. Fascinating interiors which reflect four centuries of unbroken family occupation. House Shop and fully licensed Garden Restaurant.
OPEN: MAY - SEPTEMBER, Wednesdays, Sundays, Bank Holiday Mondays and Easter Monday, 2-6pm.

Parties at other times, ring 0522-694308, or write to:
The Secretary, Doddington Hall, Lincoln LN6 4RU
Doddington is clearly signposted off the A46 Lincoln Bypass.

FULBECK HALL
on the A607 between Lincoln & Grantham Tel 0400 72205

A family home set in 11 acres of formal and wild garden For the family - picnic area, peacocks, Hebridean sheep, nature trail For the gardener - planting plans and plants for sale For everyone - a friendly, intimate house, full of interest, where you will receive a personal welcome Teas at house or Craft Workshops in Fulbeck village House and garden open Spring & Summer bank holiday Sundays and Mondays, and every day from the first to the last Sunday in July Garden open every Tuesday and Wednesday from Easter to end October All opening 2 - 5pm.

BELVOIR CASTLE

Leicestershire home of the Duke and Duchess of Rutland

The Castle commands a magnificent view over the Vale of Belvoir, and houses notable pictures, staterooms and the Museum of the 17th/21st Lancers. Special events most Sundays, including Medieval Jousting Tournaments. Adventure play area, gift shop and restaurant. The Castle is open from Easter until the end of September, and is signposted from the A1, A46, A52 and A607.

For further details contact the Estate Office, FREEPOST, Belvoir Castle, Grantham, Lincs, NG31 6BR
or telephone Grantham (0476) 870262

rooms, rising by a superb staircase to the climax of the 100ft **Long Gallery** from where there are views down on to the surrounding gardens. Regular summer concerts are held in the Gallery and there is an **embroidery exhibition** there throughout each August. There is also an entertaining house shop, while the fully licensed garden restaurant provides delicious lunches and teas.

The Hall is open on Wednesday and Sunday afternoons from May-September, and also on Bank Holiday Monday and Easter Monday. Further enquiries tel: (0522) 694308.

FULBECK HALL For elegance of quite another age, visitors may like to take the A607 to Fulbeck, where fine C18th wrought iron entrance gates announce you have reached **Fulbeck Hall**. Little can be seen from the road but go in and find the **glorious, mainly Edwardian gardens** with their terrace and yew hedges, tulip and cedar trees overlooking breathtaking views to the west - on a clear day you can see 40 miles. The gardens are being revitalised with a great deal of new and unusual planting within the original design. Planting plans can be bought or borrowed, ideal for the gardener looking for new ideas. The family have lived at Fulbeck since 1632. The present house was built by Francis Fane in 1733 after a fire gutted the old family home. The service wing of about 1600 still survives. Practically every generation has made alterations and there is fascinating variety inside, with rooms and contents of many periods, including **relics of the Duke of Wellington, The Raj and Arnhem.**

A programme of courses and seminars is run through Spring and Summer and in the Autumn. For further details contact Mrs M. Fry, Fulbeck Hall, Grantham, NG32 3JW. Tel: (0400) 72205 and ask for the **'Country House Arts' programme.** On days when teas are not being served at the house it is a pleasant walk through the churchyard and across the green to the tea room at the **Craft Workshops;** and then perhaps to explore the steep streets and greens of Fulbeck, considered by many to be the prettiest village in Lincolnshire.

Belvoir Castle

Visitors to Melton Mowbray and the Vale of Belvoir can't fail to notice the imposing structure of **Belvoir Castle** standing proudly on the only hill for miles around. The name Belvoir means beautiful view and dates back to Norman times. The first castle on this site was built by a Standard Bearer to William the Conqueror, this was demolished in the Civil War in 1645, rebuilt in 1668, but was destroyed by fire in 1816, and the present building dates from shortly after this.

Belvoir was associated with many of the bloodier episodes in English history - the Wars of the Roses, Essex's plot to kill Queen Elizabeth I, was under siege for four months in the Civil War, and more latterly the Marquis of Granby distinguished himself at the Battle of Minden, and became a good successful and popular soldier, lending his name to many hostelries in the surrounding area.

It is therefore fitting that the Castle has now become famous for the recreation of **Medieval Jousting Tournaments,** which take place seven times each season on the Castle Terrace (details of where to enquire for dates are given below). The knights and horses are dressed as in the days of jousting, the dress consisting of a tunic over which is worn chain mail or full armour and a mail balaclava over the shoulders with a helm over the head to protect the face. The weapons used include swords, axes, maces (ball and chain) and lances, and the Jousters use faithful copies of these except that they are blunted.

The objective is, of course, to entertain the public by providing as authentic a tournament as possible, and each joust is breathtakingly exciting. The performers themselves are real professionals who supply horses for films and television, and they demonstrate great skill and horsemanship. **Special events** are arranged for most Sundays during the summer season, with a variety of bands, choirs, folk dance groups and other attractions to entertain the visitor.

Belvoir Castle, **home of the Duke and Duchess of Rutland** and often seen in film and on television, is open Easter-end of September, Tuesdays, Wednesdays, Thursdays, Saturdays and Sundays, also Bank Holiday Mondays. Further information can be obtained by writing to the Estate Office, FREEPOST, Belvoir Castle, Grantham, Lincs, NG31 6BR. Tel: (0476) 870262.

CROWN HOTEL

Superb a la carte restaurant and tastefully decorated lounge bar. Indoor Swimming Pool. SPECIAL BREAKS - MINI WEEKENDS 2 minutes walk to Seacroft Golf Course. Completely refurbished, the Crown Hotel provides first class service with an ambience of quiet unobtrusiveness and efficiency in full traditional English style. Situated just 1½ miles from the town centre. All bedrooms en-suite with colour TV, telephone, tea and coffee making facilities, together with the convenience of a lift.

Drummond Road, Skegness, Lincolnshire PE25 3AB
Tel: (0754) 610760 Fax: 610847

RAC ☆☆☆ AA

The Oasby Pottery Collection
is housed in the Village Store in the picturesque village of Easby.

Over 1,200 hand-thrown and hand-decorated pieces have been selected from 30 potteries in Lincolnshire and elsewhere offering an exceptionally wide choice of design and decoration.
THE OASBY POT SHOP OASBY, GRANTHAM
TEL: CULVERTHORPE (05295) 234
(Closed on Wednesdays)

WRANGLE POTTERY & CRAFTS

Main Road, Wrangle, Boston.
Telephone (0205) 870013

POTTERY & CRAFTS MADE BY LOCAL PEOPLE

For the Special Occasion Gift you need look no further than Wrangle Crafts.
* Dried Flowers * Pot Pourri * Soft Toys * Knitwear *
* Glazed and Terracotta Indoor & Outdoor Planters *
* Large Dried Flower Room *
Also the unusual:
Appliqued Cushions and much more.
Open Tues to Sun and all Bank Holidays.
Summer opening 10a.m. to 6p.m. Winter 10a.m. to 4p.m.
Closed January.

We offer something for everyone and as car parking is no problem a visit to **Wrangle Pottery & Crafts** is a pleasure.
Situated on the A52 between Boston & Skegness.

Large Car Park at rear.

Crafts of the Area

Most rural areas of Britain have a long tradition of craftsmanship, dating from a time when the communities who lived here needed to be as near as possible self-sufficient. In this respect, Lincolnshire is no exception, and one of the greatest pleasures of visiting the County is to tour around seeking out locations where good craft products can be bought, both as gifts and as mementoes of your holiday.

Many craft workshops will also offer you the **opportunity to see the craftsperson at work**, and this often gives a very special insight into the age-old traditions of such skills as weaving, woodworking, pot throwing, metal working and many more.

It also gives an article purchased in such a workshop a unique identity, because you will have seen both how it is made and who made it. In these days of mass-production, when most items we buy are completely anonymous in terms of who made or designed them, this **stamp of personality has come to be valued anew**, and a remarkable revival of the traditional crafts has been the welcome result.

Although a potter, for instance, may make many pots in the same style, he or she will never make two exactly the same, whereas a machine process will turn out hundreds of pots that are indistinguishable one from another. This immediately confers individuality on the hand-made object. Moreover, **many craftspeople will be glad to make items specifically to your own requirements**, giving you the opportunity to take the individuality of the hand-made object one stage further.

Craft products may, at first glance, seem expensive when compared with mass-produced items but it will often be the case, of course, that many years of training and practice have gone into perfecting a certain craft, and you should expect to pay for this hard-won skill.

Do also be warned **to check the provenance of whatever you buy** very carefully. Nothing is more disappointing than getting home and realising that what you have bought as a souvenir of your visit was in fact made in some completely different part of the country - even in some cases bought in from abroad. In this context, you should note the difference between craft workshops, where the crafts on display have actually been made on the premises, and craft shops, where all that may be being offered is a selection of crafts by a number of different artists. There is no need to avoid the latter, of course. They may be excellent hunting grounds, setting you off in pursuit of further items by a particular person whose work appeals to you - only do remember to check.

One of the most ancient of all crafts is that of the potter. Vessels in which to hold food, carry water and so on have been an essential part of life from the very earliest times, and the notion that such items could be decorative as well also dates back equally far.

Those who enjoy hunting out distinctive, hand-made pottery will do well to make for the **OASBY POT SHOP**, where work by potters both locally based and from further afield is displayed. The centre of the picturesque village of Oasby is a Conservation Area and includes a number of listed stone buildings, the village itself lying mid-way between Grantham and Sleaford amid pleasant undulating countryside and being easily accessible.

John and Kate Evans, who run the village shop, established a Pottery Gallery in 1988 where they now have over 1,200 pieces of hand-thrown and hand decorated pottery. These have been carefully **selected from over 30 potteries** scattered across the country, eight of which are in Lincolnshire.

The range of pottery is considerable and includes plates, mugs, bowls, jugs, lamps and other items such as terracotta garden planters. Bringing together pottery from such a large number of potteries and from such a wide area means that the choice of design and decorative finish is unusually varied. This in turn ensures that there is something to suit all tastes and pockets, prices ranging from £1.00 to £60.00.

At Wrangle, near Boston, is another opportunity to find good pottery, made by local craftspeople, along with examples of many other traditional crafts. **WRANGLE POTTERY AND CRAFTS** offers a particularly wide range of **terracotta planters** and also has an impressive selection of **dried flowers**, as well as numerous other crafts, such as soft toys, knitwear and appliqued cushions. For a general selection of crafts from the local area, this is a good outlet to explore.

The Coachhouse

High Street, Wainfleet,
Skegness, Lincolnshire
Tel: Skegness 880191

SPECIALISING IN ANTIQUE AND REPRODUCTION PINE

LARGE & VARIED SELECTION OF CRAFTSMAN MADE SOLID WOOD FURNITURE AT COMPETITIVE PRICES

Come and spend a while browsing round our emporium, shops and showrooms, where you will find an unbelievable selection of:-

- NEW AND USED FURNISHINGS
- BYGONES ● CURIOS ● ANTIQUES
- CARPETS AND RUGS ● BRIC-A-BRAC
- POTTERY AND LOTS MORE

**Open 7 days a week Monday to Saturday
9am till 6pm
Sundays 10am till 4pm**

Call in. You'll be amazed.

Newgates Gallery Stamford

Large selection of Original Paintings Fine Creative Woodturning Victorian Painting on Cast Iron & China

Woodturning Demonstrations most Saturdays Watch unique wooden objects being made in our workshop
Choose from a wide range in our Gallery

**Corner ELM STREET/NEWGATES
near Museum STAMFORD, LINCS
Telephone Stamford (0780) 57797**

Manor Stables Craft Workshops

**Fulbeck Grantham
Telephone 0400 72779**

Come and visit one of Lincolnshire's most beautiful villages. Enjoy the attractive stone-built stables which are home to a variety of craft workshops and a showroom of high quality locally made craft, at prices to suit everyone's pocket. Pottery, Jewellery, Furniture, Dried Flowers, Walking Sticks, Leatherwork, Pictures, Gifts. See the Craftspeople at work. Commissions Accepted. In the old tack room is a coffee shop with home-made light refreshments and produce.

**OPENING HOURS:
Daily 10.30a.m. - 4.30p.m.
Closed Mondays**

The Hollies

Self Catering Country Holiday Cottages

Superb views across the marshes to the wolds. Conveniently situated on the A158, 5 minutes walk from the centre of Burgh, 5 miles from Skegness. Beautifully appointed with your comfort in mind.

Car Parking.

Ring Janet Dodsworth
Skegness
(0754) 810866

PINE TREES PARK
CARAVANS & CAMPING

One mile from Skegness on the A52 South. Quiet location, all facilities include 10amp electric hook ups. Warden on site 24 hours a day. Fishing available.

Ring Jim Dodsworth
(0754) 810866
Warden (0754) 2949

A little further up the coast is the pleasant town of Wainfleet where a visit to **THE COACHHOUSE** on the High Street, a delightful and interesting establishment, is not to be missed. Here will be found a fascinating selection of shops and showrooms, surrounding **a large courtyard filled with old farming implements,** mangles, curios and bygone machinery. These bring back memories to the older generation and are of great interest to the young.

The original coachhouse itself now contains an array of rooms selling bric a brac, pots, pans, and used goods and furniture. Further shops around the courtyard offer a vast choice of carpets, rugs, brassware, antique furniture, basketware, craft items - indeed much more than there is space here to mention.

The main business of The Coachhouse, however, is **pine furniture** and the well stocked, impressive showrooms prove this, with probably the largest selection of reproduction pine furniture in Lincolnshire. Most pieces are handmade and handwaxed, finished by skilled craftsmen in workshops on the premises. There is no admission charge to visit the Coachhouse and see the collection of implements of Lincolnshire life. Indeed, you are invited to come and spend a while browsing - and you may pick up a bargain at the same time. Please note that the Coachhouse is open 7 days a week.

Now we come to the **NEWGATES GALLERY** in Stamford, a little firm which has grown out of one small idea in a most intriguing way. **Leslie Bowler**, a champion pistol shot, was always hearing moans from fellow Pistol Club members about uncomfortable pistol grips. With his friend, **John Cooke**, eight times British Pistol Champion and Olympic shot, they devised the idea of making **Pistol Grips to measure from a hand print.** After much experimentation, they perfected the technique and orders started rolling in. **Bowlers Olympic Grips** are now known world-wide and are exported to over 30 countries. They are the only firm in the British Isles who offer this service to Target Shooters and the firm grows every year.

Fine quality walnut is used and inevitably there is a certain amount of wastage. Leslie could not bear the thought of just throwing away such lovely wood so he bought a lathe and they experimented in turning small objects which customers were quick to buy.

Both Leslie and John went on extensive courses in the art of turning and so this side of the business expanded and constant experiments are made with high class woods, producing a varied selection of vases, bowls, goblets and so on, each totally unique; nothing is ever copied. The workshop is open to the public on Saturdays when turning demonstrations are given.

In the Gallery upstairs, a large selection of woodwork is shown, together with pictures to suit all tastes, such as oils, watercolours, prints, miniatures and so on. There is also a colourful display of Victorian-type painting on iron work and ceramic plates, the distinctive style of which has proved very popular. **Everything in the gallery is hand crafted and totally British**; nothing is imported. Indeed, it is nothing more nor less than a showcase for the abundant local talent.

MANOR STABLES CRAFT WORKSHOPS are in one of the most beautiful Lincolnshire villages, Fulbeck, near Grantham. The Stables retain their original stalls which are now used as workshop units by a variety of craftspeople and the old **Tack Room** is now a coffee shop, where homemade cakes and light refreshments can be bought. On sunny days visitors can sit outside in the sheltered, flower-filled stable yard.

There are seven different craftspeople working in the Stables and a large showroom where a wide range of high quality, locally made crafts can be seen and purchased. **The Showroom** displays pottery, glass, leatherwork, paintings, silk scarves, patchwork, quilting, woodwork and other gifts.

In the units **you can watch and learn** how to weave with Anne Wood or to spin with Kathy Jackson. Bead Jewellery is made by Gill Pooley; silk and lace gifts are sewn by Linda Jones and Fran Keville; Michael Hagan makes and restores furniture; and Sue Cottingham sells dried flowers and arrangements. Homemade jams, cakes, pickles and other produce are made by Wynn Smeeton and are on sale in 'The Hedgerow' unit. You will find a warm welcome from all the craftspeople and could spend a happy, interesting morning or afternoon with them.

Meanwhile, don't forget the **Vina Cooke Museum** at Cromwell near Grantham (see 'Selected Museums to Visit'), where lovers of **hand made dolls** will find many treasures.

COBB HALL CRAFTS & TEA ROOM
ST. PAUL'S LANE BAILGATE LINCOLN

Enjoy your refreshments in an olde world setting and wander round the various craft and retail units to find an original gift.

ADJOINING CAR PARKS.

TELEPHONE: LINCOLN 527317

Foliage & Unusual plants
for the garden

hardy, coloured foliage & variegated plants, and unusual plants

open: 7 days, 10.00 – 6pm
closed: Dec, Jan and Feb

gardens open to the public
Coach parties and evening visits by arrangement.

The Dingle Nursery

Stamford Road, Pilsgate,
Stamford, Lincs PE9 3HW
Tel: (0780) 740775

located on B1443, ½ mile from Burghley House

WONDERFUL WOODTHORPE

LINCOLNSHIRE

SALES AND RENTAL OF LUXURY STATIC HOLIDAY HOMES (NEW & USED) SET IN A BEAUTIFUL COUNTRY PARK WITH EVERY AMENITY

SELF CATERING ACCOMMODATION
TOURING CARAVANS WELCOME
ALL WEATHER BOWLING GREEN - Bowling Clubs Welcome.
GOLF COURSE - Tournaments by prior arrangement.
WOODTHORPE COUNTRY INN - Bar & restaurant facility, family room open 7 days and evenings per week.
FISHING - Well stocked lake landscaped for wheelchairs.
AQUATICS - Ponds, pumps, liners, filters, fish, plants etc.
GARDEN CENTRE & COFFEE SHOP
WOODTHORPE Nr.ALFORD, LINCOLNSHIRE LN13 0DD
5 miles inland - Central to the major resorts on the East Coast - Ring for more details and colour brochure

TEL: WITHERN (0507) 450294

COBB HALL CRAFTSYARD, in Lincoln's ancient Bailgate, is another multiple crafts enterprise, also based in former stables. Here, situated below the Cobb Hall Tower in the Castle (hence the name), is **a unique complex of craft shops** offering any amount of interest for the keen craft hunter.

Upstairs, overlooking the yard, is a shop selling hand-carved, brilliantly coloured **'Smoking Men'** of all sizes and descriptions, along with German cuckoo clocks, musical boxes, roundabouts and many other unusual items, which give the shop a fascination all of its own.

The art of sugar icing can be seen in the adjacent shop and an extensive range of equipment for this most attractive craft can also be purchased. Meanwhile, Linda Makin specialises in **pressed flower arrangements**, which can be purchased in key rings, finger plates, pictures and many other items. A service in much demand is the arranging of bridal bouquets into a picture, as a constant reminder of the 'Big Day'.

Downstairs, is **Crisbens Dried Flower Shop**, where displays can be made to order, or you can buy a container and flowers of your choice from the very wide range. **Sticks and Wicks** is a specialist candle shop, with candles of every size and hue, with a wide range of matching table accessories.

Busy Hands, the largest shop in the Complex, sells craft kits for all ages, toys, and all kinds of crafts materials, including a very wide selection of exclusive tapestries, silks and wools.

Finally, **Paula Clarke's** shop is the latest shop to open, specialising in British and Continental designer wear and accessories for every occasion. And if all this choice makes you feel that you need a little time to think, why not make a visit to the **Tea Room**, and enjoy the excellent home-made fare while making up your mind.

Having mentioned dried flowers, what about living ones? The ability to produce plants in perfect condition is certainly a very demanding 'craft' and one which takes just as many years to perfect as any other skill.

In a county such as Lincolnshire, famed world wide for the excellence of its flowers, it is no surprise to find **numerous excellent garden centres.** Moreover, for all those visitors who are gardeners, whether in the flowerbeds outside or in pots on a sunny window-sill, there can be no more appropriate or pleasure-giving souvenirs of your visit to Lincolnshire than living plants. This way, you have something that changes with the seasons, lives and grows larger and more beautiful with every year that passes.

The choice of garden centres in the County is exceptional, some specialising in particular types of plant, such as herbaceous plants or conifers, while others offer plants across the whole range, as well as many practical items for the garden as well.

An excellent example of the former is the **DINGLE NURSERY**, near the historic town of Stamford, which specialises in hardy, **coloured foliage and variegated plants** for the garden, most of which are generally not available in most garden centres. Nearly all of these have flowers, which is a delightful bonus on a plant whose foliage is in any case attractive in colour and form.

A wide variety of well cared for plants are for sale and specimens can be seen growing in the gardens. All stock is well labelled and weed free. **Hardy perennials** are a speciality, but there is also a good range of **alpines, shrubs, grasses, herbs and some conifers and heathers.** Friendly staff are on hand to give advice if needed.

The Nursery is set in picturesque, landscaped grounds and visitors, who include both keen plantspeople and beginner gardeners, enjoy leisurely walks around the peaceful gardens that overlook countryside to the east of Stamford. Burghley House is close by and is usually open from Easter to October.

The Dingle Nursery is located on the B1443, 2 miles (3 kms) out of Stamford on the Barnack Road. Follow signs in Stamford for Burghley House and continue half a mile (1 km) past the main public entrance. For visitors coming from the east through Barnack, please note that the Nursery is outside Pilsgate on the Stamford Road.

The Nursery and gardens are open daily 10am-6pm, but closed in December, January and February. Evening visits and coach parties are welcome by prior arrangement, and a warm welcome for all visitors is assured.

FREE DAY OUT FOR ALL THE FAMILY

FREE DISPLAY GARDENS • FREE PETS CORNER • FREE PLAYGROUND • FREE AQUATIC AREA • FREE CAR AND BUS PARKING and of course lots of bulb, plant, tree and shrub bargains at the brightest place in gardening.

OPEN DAILY
9am - 5.30pm
WINTER.
9am - 6pm
SUMMER

Vast under cover area so wet weather won't spoil your day.

HOP-IN LICENSED RESTAURANT Hot and Cold Snacks Roast - lunch Open 9.30 - 5.00 daily and 9.30 - 5.30 weekends

BAYTREE NURSERIES GARDEN CENTRE WESTON

1 1/2 miles East of Spalding on the main A151 Spalding/Holbeach Road. Telephone 0406 370242

THE GARDEN CENTRE ASSOCIATION APPROVED MEMBER

However you arrive, by car, cycle or foot to watch or enjoy cruising angling or rambling you are sure of a Great Day Out

Bar Meals

Served daily – Noon until 2.00pm then 7.00pm until 10.00pm. Select from our wide range of delicious meals from a satisfying sandwich through Ploughmans to a scrumptious Scampi and our specialities – Chicken Curry or Cumberland Sausage. You need to see our full menu to appreciate the choice

Brandy Wharf Cider Centre

featuring

Lincolnshires Traditional Riverside Cider Tavern

Over 60 various ciders stocked including upto 18 on draught by Westons, Bulmers, Coates, Gaymers Symonds, Merrydown etc.

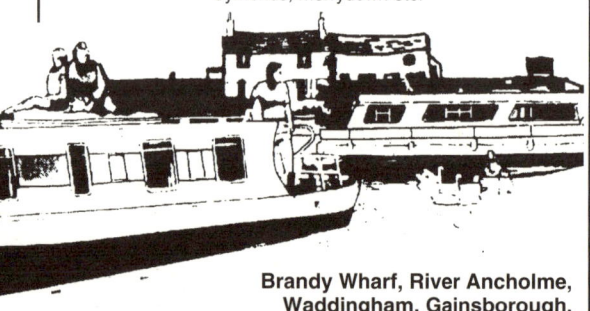

Brandy Wharf, River Ancholme, Waddingham, Gainsborough, Lincolnshire DN21 4RU. Telephone: (0652) 678364

Baytree Nurseries Garden Centre

Baytree Nurseries and Garden Centre, 2 miles (3kms) east of Spalding and just a mile (2 kms) from the famous Springfields Gardens, is worth a visit whether you are contemplating buying plants or coming to just enjoy a browse. Baytree started as a modest smallholding 21 years ago, since when, Reinhard (from Bavaria in Germany) and his Lincolnshire born wife Yvonne have become something of a legend in their own lifetime. They grow most of their own nursery stock, and, thanks to their policy of using the very latest growing techniques and equipment, their prices are considered to be some of the lowest in the country.

Among the attractions is a **Pot Plant House**, which is one of the biggest in eastern England. Seasonal changes combined with specific promotions and features of unusual or rare items make regular visits worthwhile. From Easter to October there is an **Aquatic Area** featuring everything for the water garden enthusiast from goldfish to Koi Carp, and all manner of accessories, such as pumps, liners, filters - and expert advice.

Browsing through the main shop, you will find many interesting surprises, the usual gardening requisites, plus a comprehensive book shop, country-made jams, biscuits, sweets, a gift and souvenir department. Indeed, the list is more or less endless.

'**Just for You**' is the floristry department, a member of Interflora, which stocks everything for the amateur or professional flower arranger as well as dried and fresh flowers.

Another special building is devoted to **Roses**, a Baytree speciality. Over 150 different varieties are available, including several bred by the proprietor, Reinhard Biehler, and named after his three daughters, Jutta, Gitta and Elke.

Bay Tree Nurseries and Garden Centre also offer the fully-licensed and self service **Hop-In Restaurant**, set in delightful surroundings and offering hot and cold snacks, drinks and cakes right up to full roast meals. The Centre is open daily from 9am-6pm in summer and 9am-5.30 pm in winter.

Brandy Wharf Cider Centre

The name **Brandy Wharf** conjures up many magical connotations as to its origin. Indeed folk have linked the area with smuggling. However the village name appears to have been derived from a religious sect of Viking settlers named Brande, who became stranded here after exploring this tributary of the River Humber, shortly after their invasion in 867AD. Initially the Brandes who occupied the area had self-sufficient grounds for crops, animals and enough orcharding for their own needs. They also operated a ferry service for travellers over the tidal River Ancholme, which would flood to about half mile wide with a depth of 5-9 feet (as much as 3 metres). The west bank pick-up point became known as Brande's Wharf, altered through time to its present title.

On that site the Priory of Winghall was built, only to fall into disarray and, with the Dissolution of the Monasteries in 1536 and the confiscation of religious wealth, the Priory became ruinous, finally disappearing altogether. Today, no trace remains. The word Ancholme explains that the area was the 'Home of the Anchorites', religious recluses, hermits and the like, and at one time there were many monasteries along the length of the river.

An Act of Parliament was passed in 1769 for the New River Ancholme to be excavated and lock-gates placed at South Ferriby, thus turning the quagmire into fertile arable land. By the mid 1780s Brandy Wharf was seeing many changes, with the course of the river altered, the new highway in place and several new industries setting up. The cottage, set in the midst of the orchard and occupied by Magdelene Porter, was demolished and the Tavern built to serve the needs of the navvies and bargemen. Finally, the orchard itself began to disappear.

Today you can still step back into the atmosphere of yesteryear with a visit to the Cider Centre on the upstream east bank of the New River Ancholme, adjacent to the hump-back bridge carrying the B1205 Grimsby-Caistor-Gainsborough-Midlands road. There is an infant orchard of 42 apple and pear trees, and a small though comprehensive Museum. But of course, the centre of attraction is the Tavern, where the cider experience is overwhelming - with cider pots hung from the ceilings, cider posters, drinking mugs and a display of over 60 various ciders including up to 18 on draught from around the country.

Pearoom Craft Centre

Contemporary and traditional crafts including woodcarving, ceramics, felt making, millinary and musical instrument restoration. Special workshops and events take place throughout the year.
Tea room and gallery shop.

Open daily 10.00 - 5.00, Sundays and Bank Holidays 12.00 noon - 5.00

**Station Yard, Station Road, Heckington, Nr Sleaford
Telephone: (0529) 60765**

Heckington Windmill

Situated in the delightful village of Heckington, the mill is unique as the only surviving eight sailed working mill in the country. Open daily 10.00 - 4.30 (enquire at Tourist Information in the Pearoom Craft Centre Tel (0529) 60088) Can be seen working (wind permitting) Summer weekends, Bank Holidays and Sundays during winter.

Station Road, Heckington, Nr Sleaford.

STAMFORD ANTIQUES CENTRE

in

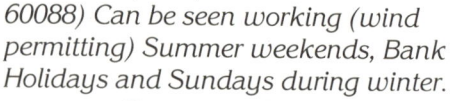

THE EXCHANGE HALL
BROAD STREET, STAMFORD
LINCS. PE9 1PX

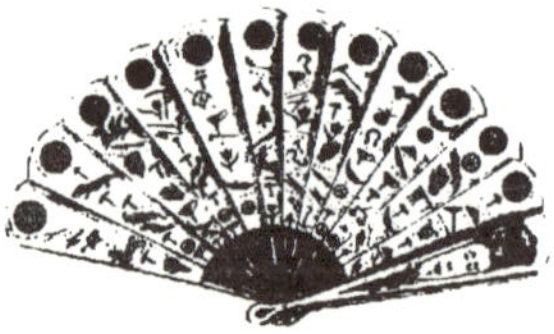

35 dealers offer a wide range of quality antiques and collectables.

Open
Monday to Thursday 10am – 5pm Friday to Saturday 10am – 5.30pm
Sunday 12 noon – 5 pm

Tel. Stamford (0780) 62605

The Pearoom Craft Centre

Another most interesting and enjoyable place to visit is **The Pearoom Craft Centre** in Heckington. So often it is the case that the buildings in which craft centres are located are themselves of much interest. Indeed, often the old character of such a building offers not only a suitable display area for crafts or antiques but also an atmosphere in which craftspeople themselves find inspiration. Moreover, this same atmosphere may be effective in inspiring visitors with a special appreciation of the items for sale, giving them new ideas of how such products might be displayed in their own homes.

The Pearoom is indeed fascinating in this respect. Built in the late 1800s, it originally belonged to a local seed firm who used it as a pea sorting warehouse. Now the building has a new lease of life as a **Heritage and Craft Centre**. On the ground and first floors are the busy workshops of the talented professional craftworkers based here.

Both traditional and contemporary, functional and decorative craftwork can be viewed, from beautiful hand carved birds and animals to ceramics and machine embroidered textiles. Elegant hand-stitched gloves and exotic and unusual hats are also displayed, together with colourful stained glass and jewellery made from precious metals.

Felt making is another unusual craft that will be discovered, and vividly coloured felted hats, bags and jackets are on show in the centre's **Gallery Shop**. You may also hear strains of music from the workshop, which specialises in the repair and restoration of brass and woodwind instruments.

On the third floor, a permanent **Heritage Exhibition** is housed, in addition to a changing programme of touring exhibitions from a wide range of contemporary craft workers and designers from all over the East Midlands.

The tea-room offers home made fayre, and the **Tourist Information Centre**, also located in th Pearoom, can advise you on the lively events that take place here regularly.

Stamford Antiques Centre

There is nothing quite like a bargain buy to make an antique collector happy, whether the object acquired is to be kept as a personal treasure or sold on for 'loadsa money'!

A visit to Stamford gives you the opportunity to visit the **Stamford Antiques Centre** on Broad Street. As has already been stressed elsewhere in this guide, Stamford is a town of quite exceptional elegance and interest, certainly meriting a visit in its own right.

The building in which the Stamford Antiques Centre is found is also a building with a fascinating past. Housed in the old **Corn Exchange**, it stands on the site of the stables of a C16th coaching Inn.

In more recent years, it was a Cinema and then a Theatre. Indeed, the Centre still closes for a week after Christmas to allow for an annual production by the Stamford Pantomime Players and for a week after Easter to allow for the Stamford Operatic Society to perform.

There are **over 35 dealers in the Centre** offering a wide range of antiques, collectables and oddities for the discerning. This really is a wonderful hunting ground if you enjoy collecting things which are old or unusual.

Especially popular are items from the **Art Deco and Art Nouveau** periods. With a general dateline of 1939, these include furniture, silver and silver plate, jewellery, porcelain, pictures and prints, books and a superb range of linen.

Along with the revival of interest in traditional crafts, which we have already noted earlier, has come a new enthusiasm for antiques and bygones. Certain television programmes have been influential in this respect and have brought the pleasures of hunting for antiques into the experience of many new purchasers. You never know, you may find something which was fashioned by a Lincolnshire craftsman a century or more ago. What is certain is that, whatever you buy here, it will always remind you of your visit to this most beautiful town.

And when you have hunted down your bargain, you can relax in the **tea room** with a coffee and homemade cake, an ideal way to round off your visit.

GROSVENOR MANOR TRADITIONAL FURNITURE LTD

.... And so much more

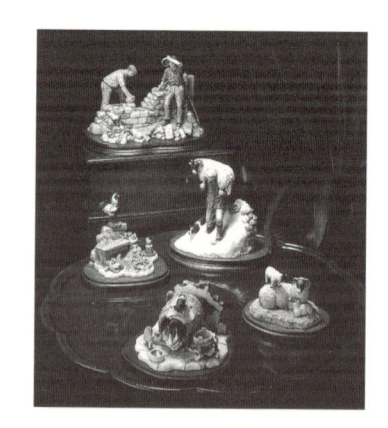

THE BROADWAY WOODHALL SPA
LINCOLNSHIRE LN10 6ST.

TELEPHONE: (0526) 52748
FURNITURE TRADITIONALLY MADE IN
Ash-Cherry-Chestnut-Mahogany-Oak-Walnut-Yewtree

BROADWAY CRAFTS & GIFTS

For handmade gifts in Lace and Pottery, many of the items are made in the shop to order. Wide selection of Pot-Pourri and Fragrance Oils. Interesting and unusual soft toys including Turtles!
Well worth a visit you'll never know what you might find!

SHOP 6 THE BROADWAY CENTRE

Grosvenor Manor

A visit to Woodhall Spa is not complete without popping in to the showrooms of **Grosvenor Manor**, situated on the Broadway next door to the Methodist Church and just a few yards from the Golf Hotel.

Grosvenor Manor is a small family business privately owned and run by Mr and Mrs M.R. Grosvenor. They specialise in traditionally made furniture and can offer a wide choice from many established family firms of **English Cabinet Makers**, using solid mahogany, solid English oak and the more unusual yew tree, cherry and walnut. Many of the smaller pieces have found their way to different parts of the country as customers take them home at the end of their holidays. Meanwhile, delivery of larger items can always be arranged.

To complement the furniture, they have carefully brought together **an extensive range of collectors' items**, all deliberately chosen from small workshops in the UK. This is a collection which they are always developing and to which they regularly add as they find hand-made items of special interest.

For instance, their latest addition is work by **local artist, Robin Wheeldon**. Robin's subjects are Lincolnshire country scenes depicting farming from a bygone era. They are currently displaying the limited edition print 'Steam Threshing', showing a steam driven threshing machine which was made by Fosters of Lincoln.

Also on show is the fascinating **art of Decoupage** by the finest exponent of the art in this country, **John Ellam**. Grosvenor Manor has the only collection of John's work in Lincolnshire. Decoupage is the Victorian art of building a lifelike picture by hand.

The **Border Fine Arts handpainted sculptures** are on display and the Grosvenors enjoy meeting society members and discussing the latest editions as well as the limited edition pieces. For the young at heart Border Fine Arts have charming studies of the Beatrix Potter characters and figures from Jill Barklem's 'Brambly Hedge' books.

Also on display are **limited edition prints** by Tony Sheath and Hilary Scoffield as well as the Portraits of Britain series by Glynn and Philip Martin. Francis Frith **photographs of old Lincolnshire** complement the fine art collection, and a good selection of desk and table lamps, mirrors, fine bone china and oven to tableware are all part of the Grosvenor Manor Collection.

You are warmly invited to browse around the showrooms in pleasant surroundings. Mr and Mrs Grosvenor look forward to meeting you.

Broadway Centre

Just follow the sound of a sewing machine whirring in the **Broadway Centre** in Woodhall Spa, and you'll find an Aladdin's cave of hand crafted treasures. Next to the Melrose Tea Room is a shop which is a delight to browse around, and one which is becoming well known to locals and visitors alike.

Behind the counter and the sewing machine is **Trixie Flint, of Branston**, who is the deft pair of hands behind the beautiful **lacework** in the shop. Trixie has been taking her work to craft shows up and down the country for 10 years, but decided that she would like a more permanent home for her work, and moved into the shop early in 1991.

She also sells **a great variety of craftwork** made by friends and acquaintances, including soft toys and puppets, from old favourites like Sooty and Sweep to newer heroes such as the Teenage Mutant Hero Turtles. Oil burners and oils and pot pourri are popular with customers and, as with all her goods, Trixie keeps the prices as low as possible.

It is the sort of shop you can visit half a dozen times and still keep finding something new - pottery, wooden toys, quilling kits, and basket-work to name but a few. The joy of this shop is the **personal service** Trixie can give. If you like an item of lace work but would like an alteration to the design, she can do it while you wait; and if you see something you like but have one or two ideas of your own, she can get your **exact requirements made to order**.

So if you are seeking an extra special gift, or just something that little bit different, why not look in on Trixie? The betting is that you won't come away empty handed.

Hemswell Antiques Centres

270 Shops in Three Adjacent Buildings
selling
Period Furniture - Shipping Furniture - Pine Furniture - Oriental Rugs - Long Case Clocks - Jewellery - Prints - Books - Silver - Pictures - Ceramics and many Collectables

Tel: Hemswell 389 (STD 042-773)　　　Open Daily 10.00a.m. to 5.00p.m.

10 miles North of Lincoln: Newark 25 miles 1 mile from Caenby Corner on the A631 to Gainsborough

Licensed Restaurant and Garden Centre

Nationwide Deliveries arranged. Container Packing Service. Single item shipping arranged.
Car Parking for 400 cars.

Hemswell Antiques Centres,
Caenby Corner Estate, Hemswell Cliff, Gainsborough, Lincs. DN21 5TJ.

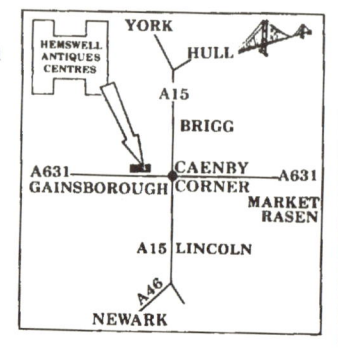

Hemswell Antiques

The chapter on the RAF in Lincolnshire explores many of the existing and former RAF stations and airfields for which the area is famous; while at the end of the Aircraft Trail, mention is made of Hemswell, as a detour which aircraft enthusiasts may like to make.

In fact, however, there are **numerous excellent reasons for making for Hemswell,** as this page will demonstrate. It is not an easy matter to decide what to do with a redundant air base, but at Hemswell Cliff a quite remarkable solution has been found, which makes a day out here well worth while.

During the First World War, Hemswell was actually known as Harpswell, and was **one of the oldest air bases in Britain**. The cricketer, Freddie Trueman, and the entertainer, Michael Bentine, were two of the very many men and women who served here during World War II.

The flying station was closed in 1965, however, and the buildings and runways quickly fell into disrepair, becoming a considerable eyesore. The barracks buildings at Caenby Corner, though despite their near-ruinous condition, caught the eye of **Rex Miller and his wife Nepi** (short for Penelope), who saw that they offered tremendous potential.

Realising the enormous attraction of antiques fairs, they had the imaginative idea that they could convert some of these buildings into what would be, in effect, a **permanent antiques fair**, thus helping dealers avoid the problem of endlessly having to pack up their goods and move them around the country, with all the hard work that that involves.

They consequently acquired the buildings from the Ministry of Defence and set about the enormous task of restoring them to a reasonable condition. Considering that there was no proper water supply, let alone any electricity or gas, this really was a major undertaking, but eventually the first rooms were ready and the first antiques dealers moved in.

The theory was that if the display was large enough, and centrally enough located, then the purchasers would come to them. Certain other factors were important, of course, above all **the need for the antiques on display to be of a very high quality.** Rex's determination that this should be so is partly based on his certainty that in the end it is the private collector to whose taste they must cater, since even trade purchasers are all looking to sell on to private collectors in the end - so quality is all-important. All objects at the Centre are, however, given a trade price and attract trade buyers from home and overseas.

To launch the Centre, **an antiques fair was held in a marquee in the grounds** and this attracted large numbers of local visitors, who soon became aware of the **magnificent antiques** hunting ground that was now on their doorstep. Several further marquee fairs have since been held and word is spreading all the time, so that more and more purchasers now realise that Hemswell Antiques is, in fact, the largest permanent selection of antiques in the UK.

The list of antiques for sale in the Centre is too long to detail here, as **some 300 dealers now occupy the buildings,** but it covers everything from small items and ornaments costing only a few pounds to large dining tables and sets of chairs, worth several thousands. **Victorian furniture**, now a major collecting interest, is strongly featured in the Centre and another popular area for collectors is furniture and **ornaments from the Art Nouveau and Art Deco periods.**

One shop which has especial appeal is the ingeniously named **Second Time Around,** where you will find a quite marvellous selection of grandfather, longcase, wall-mounted and other clocks, many by named makers and some by local specialists. **Other delights to explore include** a large selection of brass and metalware, plenty of silver plate, Victorian kitchenware, numerous prints, and paintings in both oils and watercolours, books, dolls, ceramics and a whole host of other collectables, all displayed in most attractive settings. Each sales point is manned by a sales assistant and plenty of information about the objects for sale is readily available.

In addition to the Antiques Centre, there are the remaining features of the RAF base, which will be of great interest to many visitors, a major **garden centre** where conservatories are a special feature, plenty of room for children, spacious car parking facilities and, in what was once the Officer's Mess, the luxurious **Hemswell Cliff Hotel** - the whole combination offering a marvellous day out for all.

TICs and Useful Information

TOURIST INFORMATION CENTRES

BOSTON
Blackfriars Arts Centre, Spain Lane,
PE21 6HP
Tel: (0205) 356656

BRIGG
The Buttercross, Market Place, DN20 8ER
Tel: (0652) 57053

CLEETHORPES
42 - 43 Alexander Road, DN35 8LE
Tel: (0472) 200220

GRANTHAM
The Museum, St. Peter's Hill, NG31 6PY.
Tel: (0476) 66444

GRIMSBY
Grimsby Borough Council DN31 1HU
Tel: (0472) 242000

A new TIC will be opening in the National Fishing Heritage Centre in summer 1991. Telephone number not available at the time of going to press.

HECKINGTON
The Pearoom, Centre for Contemporary Crafts, Station Yard, Sleaford, NG34 9JJ
Tel: (0529) 60088

LINCOLN
9, Castle Hill, LN1 3AA
Tel: (0522) 529828

21, Cornhill, LN5 7HB
Tel: (0522) 512971

MABLETHORPE (seasonal)
Dunes Family Entertainment Centre,
Central Promenade, LN12 1RG
Tel: (0507) 472496

NEWARK
The Ossington, Beast Market Hill,
NG24 1BD
Tel: (0636) 78962

SCUNTHORPE
Central Library, Carlton Street,
DN15 6TX
Tel: (0724) 860161

SKEGNESS (seasonal)
Embassy Centre, Grand Parade,
PE25 2UP
Tel: (0754) 4821

SPALDING
Ayscoughfee Hall, Churchgate. PE11 2RA
Tel: (0775) 725468

STAMFORD
The Museum, Broad Street, PE9 1PJ
Tel: (0780) 55611

OTHER USEFUL ADDRESSES

DESTINATION HUMBERSIDE
PO Box 80, FREEPOST, Hull,
HU6 8QD
Tel: (0482) 211400
For publicity packs on the Humberside area only, not personal tourist information. For the latter, please approach Brigg or Scunthorpe TICs.

EAST MIDLANDS TOURIST BOARD
Exchequer gate, Lincoln, LN2 1PZ
Tel: (0522) 531521

LINCOLN CITY COUNCIL
City Hall, Beaumont Fee,
LN1 1BW
Tel: (0522) 511511

LINCOLNSHIRE COUNTY COUNCIL
Recreational Services, County Offices,
Newland, LN1 1YN
Tel: (0522) 552222

THE NATIONAL TRUST
The Regional Information Officer, East Midlands Regional Office, Stable Yard, Clumber Park, Near Worksop, S80 3BE
Tel: (0909) 486411

BRITISH RAIL
Passenger Service Enquiries,
Lincoln Station.
Tel: (0522) 539502
Talking timetable Tel: (0522) 540561

BUS SERVICES
Lincoln City Transport
Tel: (0522) 534444
For services within the County, please approach Lincolnshire County Council.

HARBOURMASTER
Brayford Pool, Lincoln.
Tel: (0522) 521452

WEATHERCALL
Recorded information is available on:
Tel: (0898) 500412 (East Midlands)
Tel: (0898) 500413 (Lincolnshire and South Humberside).

Historic Houses, Castles and Gardens

Opening times may be subject to alteration. Please note that some properties open on Bank Holidays, in addition to the dates given here, while some close on Good Friday, and so on. Please always check with a TIC in the area before making a special journey. Parking is generally free but most properties charge admission.

ALFORD MANOR HOUSE Alford. Red brick Elizabethan manor house with a strikingly fine thatched roof. Normally open Monday-Friday, May-September - check locally.

ALFORD MILL Alford. Five-sail mill built in 1813 by a local millwright, Sam Oxley. It closed in 1955 and was restored in 1957. Open every Saturday, March-October and also the rest of the year if wind conditions permit.

ALKBOROUGH MAZE Alkborough. Near where the Trent joins the Humber is Julian's Bower, a turf maze probably cut by medieval monks. The adjacent Church is C11th.

AUBOURN HALL south of Lincoln. Late C16th house with wood panelling and impressive carved staircase. Open Wednesday afternoons in July and August and some Sundays. Otherwise by appointment.

AYSCOUGHFEE HALL Spalding. See 'Museums of the Area.'

BELVOIR CASTLE See 'Selected Places to Visit.'

BELTON HOUSE (NT) near Grantham. The apotheosis of Restoration architecture, Belton was designed by Sir Christopher Wren and later altered by James Wyatt. It contains innumerable treasures and is set in beautiful grounds, which contain a magnificent orangery and the Belmount Tower, a triumphal arch built in 1750. Adventure playground, boat rides and miniature railway. Open Wednesday-Sunday afternoons April-October.

BISHOP'S OLD PALACE (EH) Lincoln. The ruins of the once magnificent C13th episcopal palace, which stood adjacent to Lincoln Cathedral.

BOLINGBROKE CASTLE Old Bolingbroke near Spilsby. Scanty remains of the castle which was the birthplace of Henry IV. Open all year.

BOOTHBY PAGNELL MANOR Boothby Pagnell, south east of Grantham. Plenty of Norman castles have survived in England but very few more modest buildings, which makes this remarkably unspoilt Norman manor house, all the more precious, despite its later extensions. Enquire locally for opening times.

BROWNE'S HOSPITAL Broad Street, Stamford. This C15th hospital, one of the finest left in England, provided almshouse accommodation for ten destitute men. Its chapel is especially fine and there is an interesting historical display. Open daily Easter-October.

BURGHLEY HOUSE near Stamford. Very much on the edges of the area covered by this guide, Burghley is generally considered Britain's most magnificent Elizabethan house, home of the Cecil family for over four centuries. Its fine state rooms, of which the most famous is the breathtaking 'Heaven Room', display an excellent collection of Italian art and many interesting scientific instruments, in rooms of matchless splendour. 1991 sees a major exhibition of the Burghley collection of European ceramics, including Italian maiolica, not normally on view. The grounds have become well known to the television viewing public, as they host the annual Burghley Horse Trials three-day event each September. Open Easter to early October daily.

BROWNE'S HOSPITAL Stamford. Beautiful stained glass is an important feature of these late C15th almshouses. Open daily except Fridays, May-September.

BURGH-LE-MARSH WINDMILL west of Skegness. Also built by Sam Oxley (see Alford Mill), this mill is unusual in having left-handed sails. Open daily. Guided tours by arrangement.

CLAYTHORPE MILL near Alford. The mill serves food (booking advised) from its own smokery, which can be visited. Peacocks and a collection of domestic fowl. Open daily Easter-Christmas.

DODDINGTON HALL See 'Selected Places to Visit.'

DOGDYKE PUMPING STATION Tattershall. The only known land drainage pumping engine of its kind powered by steam. Steaming days usually on some Sundays between May and October. Enquire locally to check dates.

ELLIS MILL Mill Road, Lincoln. This late C18th four-sailed mill was largely destroyed by fire in 1973, but the Lincoln Civic Trust selected it as their Silver Jubilee Project and re-opened it, magnificently restored, in 1981. Open all weekends, April-September, and alternate weekends the rest of the year.

EPWORTH RECTORY Epworth south west of Scunthorpe. This Queen Anne House was the Wesley family home and contains various relics from the early days of Methodism. Open daily but afternoons only on Sunday, Easter-October.

FULBECK HALL See 'Selected Places to Visit.'

FYDELL HOUSE Boston. This Queen Anne house, dating from 1700, has an exceptionally beautiful staircase.

GAINSBOROUGH OLD HALL See 'Selected Places to Visit.'

GAINSTHORPE DESERTED MEDIEVAL VILLAGE 5 miles (8 kms) south west of Brigg, South Humberside. One can trace in the earthworks here the street plan and outlines of houses and gardens in the medieval village. Open all reasonable hours.

GRANTHAM HOUSE Grantham. C14th town house, updated in the mid-C18th. Open Wednesdays, April-September, by written application only.

GREEN DRAGON Waterside North, Lincoln. C14th wool merchant's house, now a very comfortable restaurant.

GRIMSTHORPE CASTLE See 'Selected Places to Visit.'

GUILDHALL Lincoln. Built over the Stonebow, one of the entrance gateways to the C15th City of Lincoln, this building houses the City Council Chamber and the Mayor's Parlour. Its display of ceremonial regalia and gifts is among the finest in the country.

GUNBY HALL near Spilsby. This attractive Queen Anne house, in red brick, has a C19th extension and contains fine English furniture and some excellent paintings. It also has a lovely garden. Open Wednesday afternoons, April-September and at other times by appointment.

HARLAXTON MANOR Grantham. Designed in the C19th by Anthony Salvin and William Burn but as a highly ornamented Jacobean manor house, Harlaxton Manor has amazing interiors and a conservatory on the grand scale. As it is part of the University of Evansville, Indiana, USA, it can only be visited by arrangement.

HARRINGTON HALL Spilsby. This C17th redbrick manor replaces a house mentioned in the Domesday Book. This is where Tennyson's Maud was invited to 'Come into the Garden...' The adjacent Church has some good ornamental brasses. Enquire locally for opening times.

HECKINGTON WINDMILL See 'Lincolnshire's Windmills.'

LINCOLN CASTLE See 'Selected Places to Visit.'

LINCOLN CATHEDRAL See 'The City of Lincoln.'

THE LION AND SNAKE Lincoln's oldest pub, located in Bailgate and built in 1640.

MARSTON HALL north of Grantham. This basically Tudor house has been the Thorold family home since the C14th. It contains period furniture and a precious collection of old master paintings, and is set in beautiful gardens which contain perhaps the largest laburnum tree in Britain. Open by appointment only.

MAUD FOSTER MILL Boston. This very tall, brick mill with its five sails is the only one still in commercial operation in Lincolnshire. Stoneground flour for sale. Open Wednesdays, Sunday afternoons and Bank Holiday Mondays all year. Usually a Vintage Weekend in July.

NORMANBY HALL AND COUNTRY PARK near Scunthorpe, South Humberside. The hall dates from the Regency period, is furnished accordingly and is set in beautiful grounds in which herds of deer are seen.

PINCHBECK ENGINE HOUSE near Spalding. An important industrial relic, this was the last working engine house, pumping water to drain the surrounding fenland, last working in 1952. There is an exhibition about land drainage and embankment. Open daily April-September and at other times by appointment.

ST MARGARET'S CHURCH Somersby near Spilsby. Tennyson's father was Rector here (the poet was born in the Old Rectory opposite). Some Tennyson memorabilia.

ST MARY'S GUILDHALL Lincoln. Lincoln Civic Trust are restoring this C12th building beneath whose floor can be seen a stretch of the Roman Fosse Way! Open the fourth Sunday afternoon of each month, April-September or by appointment. Do not confuse with the Guildhall (see above).

ST PETER'S CHURCH Markby. There was once a famous Augustinian Priory here, built around 1160 but destroyed in the Dissolution of the Monasteries. What survives today is this charming and interesting church, built from the Priory ruins in the early C16th and the only thatched church in the County.

STOKE ROCHFORD HALL south of Grantham. Like Harlaxton Manor, a magnificent C19th house designed in Jacobean style. It is now a luxury conference centre owned by the National Union of Teachers, in very beautiful grounds.

TATTERSHALL CASTLE (NT) between Sleaford and Horncastle. This wonderful mid-C15th tower house, in red brick with details in stone, was built in 1440 by Ralph Cromwell, Lord Treasurer of England. The turret rooms contain recently updated displays and there is a small shop. Open daily all year.

THORNTON ABBEY Ulceby, between Scunthorpe and Grimsby. The extremely imposing redbrick gatehouse gives a good impression of this C12th Augustinian foundation, one of the most powerful of the land, but destroyed at the time of the Dissolution of the Monasteries (1536-40). Of the Church itself, built in stone, there are fairly limited remains. Open daily, Easter to mid-October, weekends only rest of year.

WALTHAM MILL near Cleethorpes. Imposing tower mill and small agriculture museum. Check times locally.

WOOLSTHORPE MANOR (NT) Woolsthorpe-by-Colsterworth, south of Grantham. This charming C17th house was where Sir Isaac Newton was born on Christmas Day in 1642. In his study is a reconstruction of the experiment that helped him work out the prismatic colour sequence, while in the garden is the very tree from which, tradition has it, the apple fell on to the great man's head and revealed to him the principle of gravity. Open Wednesday-Sunday afternoons, Easter-October.

WRAWBY MILL near Brigg, east of Scunthorpe. One of the last surviving post-mills in Europe. Restricted opening times, check locally.

Gardens of the Area

In the list of historic houses above, the following also have notable gardens:

AYSCOUGHFEE HALL Yew trees cut into strange shapes line the walks through this walled garden, with bedding displays, rose garden, fishpond and fountains.

BELTON HALL Impressive landscaped grounds surround several formal gardens, including an Italian Garden, a Dutch garden with clipped yews, a statue walk and the wonderful orangery, now restored, by Jeffrey Wyatville.

BURGHLEY HALL Capability Brown parkland, a good example of landscaping on the grand scale, with lake, stables, orangery, ice house, summer house etc.

FULBECK HALL Terraced gardens with ancient trees and a series of recently replanted informal gardens. Many interesting plants. Wild garden and nature trail.

GRIMSTHORPE CASTLE Yew hedges divide a series of gardens, including topiary rose gardens, knot garden, geometric kitchen garden, arboretum and parkland.

GUNBY HALL Outstanding walled gardens with too many features to detail here, entirely living up to being the subject of Tennyson's 'Haunt of Ancient Peace.' Probably the most interesting garden in Lincolnshire in terms of garden design.

MARSTON HALL A series of small gardens divided by walls and hedges, connected to the landscaped park beyond by an avenue of Lombardy poplars.

Finally, TICs have details of private gardens open occasionally in aid of the National Gardens Scheme.

Museums and Nature Reserves

Most of the following are open daily in season, but please check at TICs before making a special journey.

ALLIED FORCES MILITARY MUSEUM Stickford, Boston. A private collection of miltaria, including several vehicles, mostly from World War II. Open Monday to Friday (weekends by arrangement only).

ANWICK FORGE near Sleaford. Working forge in historic C18th round house.

AVIATION HERITAGE CENTRE The Airfield, East Kirkby, Spilsby. See 'The RAF in Lincolnshire.'

AYSCOUGHFEE HALL MUSEUM OF SOUTH HOLLAND Spalding. New displays on land reclamation, gardening and the history of the area, beautifully presented to bring the history of the South Holland area to life.

BATTLE OF BRITAIN MEMORIAL FLIGHT See 'The RAF in Lincolnshire.'

BAYSGARTH HOUSE MUSEUM Barton-upon-Humber, South Humberside. Part of the Baysgarth Leisure Park, set in the grounds of Baysgarth House. There are geological and archaeological exhibits (some fine fossils), period interiors, reconstructed shops and a good collection of C18th and C19th English and Oriental ceramics. Baysgarth Cottage contains the new Rural Crafts Museum and a Museum of Local Industries will eventually occupy the Stable Block. Normally open Thursdays to Sundays all year.

BOSTON GUILDHALL MUSEUM See 'Selected Museums to Visit.'

BRANSTON RAILWAY MUSEUM Station Road, Branston. Having come to Lincolnshire only recently, from Bath, this private collection of railwayana focusses mainly on the West Country - but local items are being added. Open by prior appointment only.

CITY AND COUNTY MUSEUM Lincoln. See 'Selected Museums to Visit.'

CHURCH FARM MUSEUM Skegness. See 'The County of Lincolnshire.'

GAINSBOROUGH MODEL RAILWAY SOCIETY Much more than just a sizeable model railway layout, this is probably the largest railway of its kind, a 'working museum' illustrating the great days of steam on the LNER London to Leeds line. Limited opening, tel;: (0652) 54657.

GRANTHAM MUSEUM See 'The County of Lincolnshire.'

IMMINGHAM MUSEUM AND GALLERY Immingham, South Humberside. The Great Central Railway was an important feature of the area, as this museum recounts. Natural history displays and a chemist's shop interior too. Work by local artists displayed in the Gallery. Being extended in 1991, so check opening.

IRON AGE SETTLEMENT Weelsby Avenue, Grimsby, South Humberside. A reconstruction of a small Iron Age settlement. Open Tuesday-Saturday.

INCREDIBLY FANTASTIC OLD TOY SHOW 26 Westgate, Lincoln. Treasures from nurseries going back to 1850, a delight for children and 'never ending children', Open daily except Monday, Easter-Christmas but afternoons only on Sundays.

LINCOLN CATHEDRAL LIBRARIES Currently being restored to their former glory are these two important collections of rare books, some in the Medieval Library of 1420, the rest in the Wren Library, designed by Sir Christopher Wren in 1674.

LINCOLN CITY LIBRARY The main library in Lincoln also houses the Tennyson Research Centre, one of the most important collections on the poet in the World.

THE LINCOLNSHIRE ARCHIVES Lincoln Castle. Here are the cream of Lincolnshire's historical records, housed in a former Victorian gaol.

LINCOLNSHIRE RAILWAY MUSEUM Burgh le Marsh Station, Skegness. A true nostalgia trip for the lover of steam railways, housed in the former Goods Depot and displaying locomotives, ticket office, station master's office and signal box, along with a mass of smaller items. Also a narrow gauge passenger railway. Open daily except Mondays, June-August. Also closed on Tuesdays in September. Otherwise limited opening.

LINCOLNSHIRE VINTAGE VEHICLE SOCIETY Whisby Road, off Doddington Road, Lincoln. If you are more interested in the history of road rather than rail travel, this one is for you. Several old vehicles always being restored. Open Sunday afternoons May-September.

LOUTH MUSEUM 4 Broadbank, Louth. Louth carpets and a Louth blunderbuss feature in this collection of local relics and photographs, along with a fine collection of butterflies and moths and some Tennyson items. Limited opening, enquire locally.

MANOR HOUSE FOLK MUSEUM Alford. Domestic bygones in an attractive small museum at this historic house. Period interiors include a schoolroom, nursery, police cell, chemist and cobbler's shop. Features on Captain John Smith and Thomas Payne. Open Monday-Friday, May-September.

MAWTHORPE MUSEUM near Alford. Farming bygones, including waggons, tractors, steam engines and farming tools. Fairground organ and working model of a fairground. Limited opening, enquire locally.

MUSEUM OF LINCOLNSHIRE LIFE Lincoln. See 'Selected Museums to Visit.'

NATIONAL BEE-KEEPING MUSEUM same location as the Aviation Heritage Centre (see above). Open daily but closes at 3pm in winter months.

NATIONAL CYCLE MUSEUM Brayford Wharf North, Lincoln. The first 'bone-shakers' date from the 1820s, soon superseded by the famous Penny Farthing and eventually developing into the modern racing bikes and mountain bikes of today - and they are all here, in Britain's best cycling collection. Open daily all year.

NEWARK MUSEUM See 'Newark and Sherwood'.

NEWTON NEWTON NATIONAL FLAG CENTRE Rutland Road, Skegness. Here flags for everything from Regimental banners to Students' Union flags are made, using a host of decorative techniques. Open all weekdays. Admission includes tea or coffee and biscuits!

NORMANBY PARK FARMING MUSEUM near Scunthorpe, South Humberside. A new museum of farming life in this area, opened by HRH the Duchess of York. See also 'Historic Sites.'

NORTHCOTE HEAVY HORSE CENTRE Interesting collection of horse-drawn vehicles and much more - see 'Places for Animal Lovers to Visit.'

OLD VICARAGE MUSEUM Billinghay, north east of Sleaford. The very modest original Vicarage, a 'mud and stud' building of the early C17th, survives here, though superseded by a later building. It is currently being restored. In the workshop is local blacksmith, Ian Caudwell. Open reasonable hours when foreman is present.

PINCHBECK ENGINE AND LAND DRAINAGE MUSEUM See 'South Holland and the Fens'.

RUTLAND COTTAGE MUSIC MUSEUM Whaplode St Catherine near Spalding. See 'Selected Museums to Visit.'

SALTERSFORD MUSEUM Grantham. This C19th Waterworks building makes a good home for displays on the history of the Saltersford area. Slide presentation. The Ruston engine (1935) runs on open days - enquire locally for dates.

SCUNTHORPE MUSEUM AND ART GALLERY Oswald Road, South Humberside. Award-winning museum of local history, with many interesting displays, including a typical C19th ironworker's cottage. Regular art and craft exhibitions. Open daily but afternoons only on Sundays.

SOCIETY FOR LINCOLNSHIRE HISTORY AND ARCHAEOLOGY Steep Hill, Lincoln. In one of Lincoln's oldest streets is this Society, organising lectures, tours and fieldwork and running a local history bookshop. The building it occupies is Jews' Court which, with the adjacent Jews' House, is among the most important C12th domestic architecture in England.

SPALDING MUSEUM Broad Street, Spalding. Glass and china, medals, coins and other local relics. Open by appointment with the curator.

STAMFORD MUSEUM Broad Street. This is an interesting museum of local history and archaeology, including the real clothes worn by both the mountainous Daniel Lambert and the minuscule General Tom Thumb!

STAMFORD BREWERY MUSEUM See 'Selected Museums to Visit'.

USHER GALLERY Lincoln. See 'Selected Museums to Visit - Museums in the City of Lincoln.''

WELHOLME GALLERIES Great Grimsby, South Humberside. Once a Congregational Chapel, this building now houses a local history museum, with fine collections of ship models and sea pictures. Regular touring exhibitions. Open Tuesday-Saturday.

WILLOUGHBY MEMORIAL TRUST GALLERY Corby Glen, Grantham. C17th Grammar School now houses a library and art gallery, with changing exhibitions. Enquire locally for details.

WOODHALL SPA COTTAGE MUSEUM Iddesleigh Road, Woodhall Spa. A turn-of-the-century photographer occupied this bungalow, where the history of this typical Victorian Spa is now displayed. Open weekends, Easter-September.

WORKSOP MUSEUM See 'Boston and the Bassetlaw District'.

Nature Reserves & Country Parks

A list of sites administered by the Royal Society for Nature Conservation in Lincolnshire, is found in that organisation's own handbook. In this context, see also 'Attractions for Animal Lovers'

BARTON CLAY PITS near Barton-upon-Humber. The southbank of the Humber, with reed beds and open water walks through the Humber Wild Life Refuge. Information Centre and guided walks in summer.

BRANSBY HOME OF REST FOR HORSES near Saxilby. Rescued horses, ponies and donkeys, on view every day.

BUTTERFLY PARK Long Sutton near Spalding. Butterfly House, Insectarium, Bee Garden, Herb Garden, Farm Walk, Nature Trail, adventure playground, tea room and shop. Open daily mid-March to end of October.

ELSHAM COUNTRY PARK near Brigg, South Humberside. See 'Selected Leisure Activities'.

GIBRALTAR POINT Skegness. Probably the best place to see the combination of sand dunes and saltmarshes, with their fascinating range of plants, insects, and wading and migratory birds, some very rare indeed. Visitor Centre open daily May-October and weekends rest of year.

HARTSHOLME COUNTRY PARK Skellingthorpe Road, Lincoln. Though within the City boundary, there is plenty of wildlife to enjoy here. Information Centre (closed Wednesdays and Thursdays, and entirely closed November-February) in the Stable Block, with natural history displays, cafe (April-September), aviary, lakeside and woodland walks. Fishing. Open daily.

MESSINGHAM SAND QUARRIES NATURE RESERVE south of Scunthorpe. A combination of heath, woodland and water, welcoming countless waders, ducks and geese in winter and offering a home to numerous interesting butterflies and moths.

NORMANBY HALL COUNTRY PARK near Scunthorpe. See 'Historic Sites' and 'Museums of the Area.'

RED HILL NATURE RESERVE north of Horncastle. Disused chalk quarry, showing both red and white chalk and other layers of the Wolds rocks, a paradise for geologists. Rare plants and, for once, a fine view, from Red Hill.

SALTFLEETBY-THEDDLETHORPE DUNES nearly 5 miles (8 kms) of coastline between Saltfleet Haven and Mablethorpe. This is the only place where the natterjack toad is found in Lincolnshire, along with a whole host of other interesting fauna and flora. Sand dunes, mudflats and marshes (both salt and freshwater) support a wonderful range of rare plants and wading birds, the latter at their most interesting during winter migrations.

SNIPE DALES COUNTRY PARK AND NATURE RESERVE Featured in 'Walk Two.'

TETNEY HAVEN near Cleethorpes. RSPB Reserve with multitudinous seabirds. By appointment only.

THE TROPICAL BUTTERFLY GARDEN AND MINI BEASTS ZOO The Boating Lake, Cleethorpes. Lives up to its name, with a snack bar and gift shop as well. Open daily all year.

Towns and Villages

ALFORD This attractive market town south west of Mablethorpe contains a number of most appealing buildings, especially the thatched Manor House Folk Museum, which is mentioned in the Domesday Book, though its present appearance is Mid-C17th. Alford's fine Church, dedicated to St Wilfrid and dating from the C14th, replaced an earlier Norman building. The dark stonework of the sturdy tower contrasts with the lighter colouring of the delicate pinnacles that surmount it. Meanwhile the five-sailed windmill is one of Lincolnshire's most elegant, dating from 1813 and now restored to full working order. Alford has made a name for itself in recent years as a centre of craftsmanship and there are regular craft markets every Friday. Craft weekends bring many people to the town to enjoy displays of Morris dancing, traditional folk music and other entertainments. Tennyson's birthplace at Somersby is not far away.

ALKBOROUGH This breezy, lonely village stands overlooking the point where the Trent and the Ouse merge to become the Humber, and very fine views from the Norman church tower survey Lincoln Cathedral but also look across the Humber to Beverley and York Minsters too. Also of Norman date is the curious 'ground' maze, cut by the monks at the place called Julian Bower.

ANCASTER The town grew up in this spot as it was one of the points where the Lincoln Edge could be crossed. A large Roman camp stood nearby, on Ermine Street, at a place called Causennae, and finds from this site can be seen in Grantham Museum. Two stone coffins in the churchyard are thought to be Roman.

BARDNEY This not especially remarkable town beside the River Witham once had a truly magnificent Abbey, founded in the C7th by King Ethelred of Mercia. Viking raiders destroyed it in 870 but it was rebuilt by the Normans, only to be destroyed again at the Dissolution.

BOSTON Standing to the north side of The Wash, Boston is dominated by the beautiful tower of its Church of St Botolph, most inappropriately known locally as 'The Stump.' The Church dates from the C14th, and on Wednesdays you can mount the spiral staircase up the Stump to gain marvellous views over the surrounding fenland. There are numerous interesting old buildings. Some are of very early date, such as the ancient C13th Blackfriars (now an Arts Centre), Church Key, a charming black and white cottage and the fine timber-framed Pescod Hall. Others have the elegance of a later age, such as Fydell House, which contains an American Room, dating from 1700, and the Sam Newson Music Centre, occupying an C18th warehouse. The most celebrated, however, is the Guildhall, where the Pilgrim Fathers were tried and imprisoned after their abortive attempt to leave Boston for Holland in 1607. They succeeded twenty-three years later, in 1630, and despite their earlier ordeal they still named the town in which they settled, in Massachusetts, USA, 'Boston.' Sir Joseph Banks, the famous botanist who sailed with Captain James Cook in the 'Endeavour' to Australia, came from Boston. Other reasons for coming to Boston are the marvellously colourful bulb fields to the south of the town, the Maud Foster Windmill, the nearby fishing and boating opportunities and the excellent Peter Paine Sports Centre.

BOURNE The Augustinian Abbey here is mainly famous now for having been the place where Robert Mannyng translated various religious texts from French into English in the C12th, thus greatly advancing the development of the English language. The town is also thought to have been the birthplace of Hereward the Wake. A curious old tradition decides who holds White Bread Meadow for the year: an Auction is held while a race is run by schoolboys across the meadow, the successful bidder being whoever has made the highest offer at the moment the race is won. There is a magnificent sports ground and fine swimming pool.

BURGH LE MARSH This small town lies inland from Skegness and has a fine Church, dedicated to St Peter and St Paul, and the excellent Dobson's Windmill. Here there is a small Milling Museum, while the old Station houses the Lincolnshire Railway Museum. Much of the attractiveness of Burgh le Marsh lies in the lovely countryside which surrounds it, offering pleasant riverside walks, fishing and various leisure activities.

CANWICK Lying only a short distance to the south east of Lincoln, this village is mainly worth visiting for the views it affords of the Cathedral. It does have an interesting Norman church of its own, however, even though it has been much restored.

CASTLE BYTHAM This delightful village in the South Kesteven area has a Norman Church, whose sundial on the Tower carries the curious punning inscription, 'Bee in Thyme.' The ladder which leads up into the belfry was once the village maypole, as the record says, 'This ware the Maypoul 1660.' On the opposite side of the river are the earthworks of a great castle once owned by Morcar, brother of King Harold (note Morkery Wood, also in the vicinity) and seized by William the Conqueror's brother, Odo, who completed it. Henry III destroyed it in 1221 and its replacement fell victim to the Wars of the Roses. The Village became a Conservation Area in 1973. In the Holywell Hall area are pleasant walks.

CLEETHORPES This resort has grown, inside a century, from a little fishing village to one of Britain's most popular seaside holiday destinations. The sandy beach is 3 miles (5 kms) long and the entertainments on offer here include everything from Gandey's Circus to the Jungle World indoor tropical garden. Waltham Windmill and Hall Farm at Ashby cum Fenby are not far away. Sporting and leisure facilities are almost limitless. Boating, water-skiing, windsurfing, mini golf, putting, snooker, horse riding - you can do them all here. And you can do the really traditional seaside things too, like ride a donkey, go to the funfair and enjoy the nightlife on the pier. A major attraction in Cleethorpes is Fantasy World, opened in 1989 and already becoming established as a very popular venue for children's parties. Among the numerous delights are the Adventure Castle, with its choice of slides, the Bugs Bunny Bouncer and the Soft Play area for younger children. There is a very well-stocked cafeteria and sweet shop, and the panoramic sea views over the Humber Estuary can be enjoyed with the aid of telescopes. Fantasy World is next door to Cleethorpes Railway Station, where there is ample parking, and is open every day except Christmas Day.

CONINGSBY This village near Tattershall is in the true Fenland, the tower of its C15th Church dominating from all sides. Its clock face is the largest in the world. One of Coningsby's rectors was Laurence Eusdon, who became, in the late C18th, one of the several Poets Laureate of whom, at this later remove, no-one has ever heard! At nearby Tumby is a lovely old wood where pleasant walks can be enjoyed.

CORBY South east of Grantham, Corby has become noted for its church only relatively recently - because, when they restored it in 1939, they uncovered some of the finest medieval wall paintings in Britain.

CROWLAND Just into the south of the County, this is where St Guthlac lived as a hermit in the late C7th and the great Benedictine Abbey was later built in his memory. The ruins are still very fine. A much photographed relic is the curious - and now stranded - triangular bridge, with its carved figure of God cradling the world in his arms (perhaps?), reminding us that the water level was once much higher than it is today.

DONINGTON This village south west of Boston was where the explorer, Matthew Flinders was born in 1774. He is always said to have been inspired to go to sea by reading Defoe's 'Robinson Crusoe.' The C14th tower of the Church is very fine and the cobbled market place is most attractive. Horse and cattle fairs are still held, but Donington's main importance in the past was as a centre for the trading of flax and hemp.

EDENHAM This spectacular village is entirely in keeping with Lincolnshire's grandest stately home which stands here, Grimsthorpe Castle. In the Church are the magnificent tombs of the Willoughby de Eresby family, while the rectory is supposed to be where Charles Kingsley wrote 'Hereward the Wake.'

EPWORTH This village in the Isle of Axholme area was the birthplace of brothers John and Charles Wesley, founders of Methodism and the authors of many of our best-known hymns.

GAINSBOROUGH This village on the River Trent is mainly notable for the marvellous Gainsborough Old Hall, described in detail elsewhere in this book. George Eliot used it as the basis for St Ogg's in 'The Mill on the Floss'.

GRANTHAM Here there is yet another magnificent church with a marvellous spire, St Wulfram's. Grantham House, property of the National Trust, is sometimes open to the public, and many other historic houses, notably Belton House, Harlaxton Manor and Belvoir Castle, are not far away. The local Museum has displays on both Sir Isaac Newton, of nearby Woolsthorpe Hall, and the famous Grantham grocer's daughter, Margaret Thatcher. There is an attractive riverside walk and, right round the town, the so-called 'Gingerbread Way.' There is also a fine Leisure Centre - and Grantham remains what it has always been, a stopping place on the Great North Road.

GRIMSBY Grimsby is known worldwide as a fishing port and it still carries out that function today, being Lincolnshire's biggest town and having the largest fish market in the world. It is an invigorating mix of the old and the new, combining several very early churches, such as the C13th St James' Parish Church, the Saxon church of St Giles at Scartho and St Mary the Virgin at Old Clee. A new attraction goes back to an even earlier age, and is a re-creation of an Iron Age village. There are fine Victorian and Edwardian buildings too, and a dockland area which is being excitingly re-developed and which already has its central focus the National Fishing Heritage Centre. Shopping facilities are excellent and the town also has marvellous leisure facilities, providing the whole range of sporting and leisure opportunities.

HEMSWELL This RAF village north of Lincoln is popular with visitors for its massive Antiques Centre, as well as for the curiously nostalgic atmosphere its rows of buildings engender in those who can remember the wartime years.

HORNCASTLE This town really owes its origins to the Romans, for whom it was a garrison town for the Ninth Legion. There are still some traces of the Roman Wall to be seen, but today it is a good-looking market town, with a fine Church and some very pretty houses, among them the home, in the Market Place, of Sir Joseph Banks. It is increasingly popular as a centre of antiques shops.

INGOLDMELLS Home of the very first Butlins Holiday Resort, now converted into Funcoast World.

LINCOLN Featured in detail elsewhere in this guide.

LOUTH This neat and pretty market town is a quiet place of many charms. Its origins go back to before the Romans, though it developed most noticeably under the Danes. Among the pupils at its Grammar School were the Tennyson brothers. St James's Church, which is where the sermon that inspired the ill-fated 'Pilgrimage of Grace' was preached, has a beautifully elegant spire; and the town has many attractive houses as well as fine recreational facilities and plenty of green spaces along the River Lud (from which the name 'Louth' comes) to enjoy.

MABLETHORPE 'Mablethorpe Magic' is one slogan with which this very popular small seaside resort promotes itself, a place to enjoy the sea, the sands and all the entertainments which go with the traditional British seaside holiday. The Animal Gardens at North End are an especial attraction, and there is plenty to enjoy in the way of sport, leisure and entertainment. You could be forgiven for not realising, however, that Mablethorpe traces its origins back to Roman times - its medieval Church, for instance, was long since clawed into the sea and some tragic floods have been experienced - but in general Mablethorpe is just one of those places in which to relax and be happy. Its annual Carnival is held in August and there are other events throughout the season.

MARKET RASEN Set on the River Rase, Market Rasen traces its origins back to Saxon times and has a fine Norman Parish Church. It is best known for being Lincolnshire's only racecourse, providing a great day out for all who enjoy the 'Sport of Kings.' Also very popular, however, is the now celebrated Festival of Music, Speech and Drama, first launched in 1943.

NORTON DISNEY This lovely village, on the banks of the River Witham north east of Newark, is a special place. Its Church of St Peter, mainly in Early English Decorated style, contains the numerous very interesting tombs of the Disney family.

OLD BOLINGBROKE Here, not far from Spilsby, stood the fine Norman Castle in which Henry Bolingbroke, later Henry IV, was born. His parents were John of Gaunt and his wife Blanche - and John of Gaunt's parents were Edward III and Queen Philippa, who are probably represented by the two very worn stone heads carved beside the doorway of the ancient Church of St Peter and St Paul.

SALTFLEET This coastal village was once an important port but has lost several of its buildings to the sea, including the Church. Many others survive, however, among them the very pretty Manor House, which apparently contains what is thought to be the oldest wallpaper in Britain!

SCUNTHORPE In South Humberside, this well known industrial town is working hard to change its image. After all, only one of the many steelworks now remains and the sites where some of the others stood are being converted into marvellous parks and gardens - and as if that weren't enough, Normanby Hall and Country Park is on the outskirts of the town and Elsham Hall Country Park at Brigg is not far away either. Both of these have 18-hole golf courses, incidentally, as does Scunthorpe itself. The town has several interesting churches, the oldest being St Lawrence's, dating from the C12th and the oldest building in the town. A Scunthorpe Heritage Trail leaflet is available from the TIC. Scunthorpe has remarkable modern facilities too, however, including the very active Civic Theatre, the Majestic Cinema, the excellent Museum and Art Gallery and a splendid Caribbean-style swimming pool as part of the recently built Leisure Centre.

SKEGNESS Known to its many friends as 'Skeggy', this much loved seaside town offers everything that a holiday resort should have. In fact, however, it has been an important small port from centuries before the holidaymakers ever arrived. The details of all its leisure facilities, sporting opportunities, night time entertainments and so on are too numerous to list here, but they range from the Natureland Marine Zoo and Seal Sanctuary to a non-stop funfair and the Earl of Scarborough Sports Centre. The annual illuminations are especially popular and draw many visitors.

SLEAFORD Research shows that Sleaford is probably Lincolnshire's oldest town, dating certainly from the Iron Age. In the C11th it was one of the gifts bestowed upon Remigius, Bishop of Lincoln, and it received its market charter as early as 1202. The Parish Church of Saint Denis is as grand and beautiful as befits a settlement of such antiquity. Its tower was one of the first to have a spire added to it, but the Church's special perfection is in the delicacy of the stone carving around its windows. Other notable buildings include the C17th Carre Hospital, a row of almshouses; and the extraordinary Maltings, built at the turn of the century with foundations apparently 55 metres (180 feet) deep! For all its antiquity, the town has modern recreational facilities too and is a most pleasant place to visit.

SOMERSBY This fairly typical Wolds village has become something of a place of literary pilgrimage, for the poet Tennyson was born here in the old rectory, which can still be seen from the outside but not visited. The church, however, has a few interesting Tennyson relics.

SPALDING Best known for its bulb growing, Spalding amazes many visitors by being a town of great age, having originally grown up around the Benedictine Priory which was founded here in 1052 by Harold of Buckendale, who may have been Lady Godiva's brother. Ayscoughfee Hall (pronounced, for those who are wondering, 'Ascuffee') was the home of the founder of the Spalding Gentlemen's Society and is a very lovely old building, dating originally from the C15th and today housing the new Museum of South Holland. The River Welland, with its colourful narrowboats, runs through the town, and the Castle Sports Complex and Leisure Centre offers a fine swimming pool and other sporting facilities. Bulb growing is, indeed, the town's most important present-day industry, with the emphasis being on daffodils and tulips, seen to extraordinary effect in the annual flower parade each May.

SPILSBY This is another very appealing market town on the edge of the Lincolnshire Wolds. Children dance round the maypole here on May Day, when there is also an annual Carnival. The remains of Bolingbroke Castle are to be found here, as is the not by any means ruined - indeed very beautiful - Harrington Hall. The sturdy Church of St James is an engaging building, famous for its Willoughby de Eresby family tombs, while recreational facilities include the lovely Snipe Dales Nature Reserve and Country Park, featured elsewhere in this book.

STAMFORD After listing so many attractive market towns, it is hard to find anything to say that will do justice to Stamford, probably justly entitled 'The Best Stone Town in England.' Its beautiful buildings range mostly from medieval times to the Georgian era and, despite the centuries that separate them, they seem to harmonise to perfection. No intrusions from either the C19th, the age of the Industrial Revolution, or our own C20th have been allowed to spoil Stamford. Treasured buildings include five medieval churches, a C12th Priory and the splendid almshouses known as Browne's Hospital, dating from 1475. The town has its own interesting Museum, as well as the fascinating Steam Brewery Museum and the delightful Tolethorpe Hall, venue for the open air performances of the Stamford Shakespeare Company. Several good town trail leaflets are available from the Tourist Information Centre.

TATTERSHALL This modest village, near to the confluence of the River Bain and the River Witham, is famous for its astounding redbrick Castle, home of the Cromwell family. It is a single, massive tower, dating from the C15th, and is now owned by the National Trust.

WAINFLEET There was once an old Roman town here, from which Wainfleet takes its name, 'Vainona.' Strictly speaking called Wainfleet All Saints, it was once a thriving port, even though it is now some miles from the sea, and it delights in two lovely Parish Churches as it is really a combination of two old villages. You can hire a boat and explore the lazily meandering Steeping River, go fishing, go walking, or investigate the nearby Nature Reserve at Gibraltar Point. The town's most famous son is William of Wayneflete, Bishop of Winchester and founder of Magdalen College, Oxford. He founded a school here in Wainfleet, also called Magdalen College.

WELL VALE This beautiful, rather secret place on the eastern edges of the Wolds is but a small hamlet surrounding a stately home named Well Vale Hall, of Georgian design and not open to the public. The little Church is Classical in design.

WOODHALL SPA This enjoyable town is just what it sounds like, a kind of inland resort, surrounded by lovely farmland and woods. The Cottage Museum is one attraction, as is the remarkable Kinema in the Woods, where showings of the latest films are prefaced by performances on the splendid theatre organ, but probably what draws more visitors than anything else is the exceptionally good golf course. In fact, however, there are plenty of other things to do too, including tennis, bowls and a magnificent open air swimming pool. The beneficial spa waters were only discovered as the result of an unsuccessful attempt to mine for coal, and the town's prosperity was built on its success as a health resort for people suffering from rheumatism, arthritis and similar conditions. Today, with its fine Jubilee Park and the nearby woods, it remains a true 'garden resort.'

Advertisers' Index

HOTELS
Crest Hotel, Grimsby — 6
Crown Hotel, Skegness — 74
The Lodge Hotel, Lincoln — 28
Red Lion Hotel, Spalding — 68

GUEST HOUSES
Blaydon Guest House, Stamford — 40

BED & BREAKFAST
Village Shop & Post Office, Hough on the Hill, Grantham — 28

SELF CATERING ACCOMMODATION
The Hollies, Skegness — 76

CARAVAN & CAMPING SITES
Pine Trees Park, Skegness — 76

INN FOOD & REFRESHMENT
The Ship Inn, Pinchbeck, Spalding — 70

HOLIDAY PARKS
Bainland Country Park, Woodhall Spa — 28
Tattershall Park Country Club, Tattershall — 40
Woodthorpe Hall, Woodthorpe, Nr Alford — 78

CRAFTS & CRAFTSMEN
Broadway Crafts & Gifts, Woodhall Spa — 84
Cobb Hall Crafts & Tea Room, Bailgate — 78
Grosvenor Manor, Woodhall Spa — 84
Manor Stables Craft Workshops, Fulbeck, Grantham — 76
Oasby Pot Shop, Oasby, Grantham — 74
Pearoom Craft Centre, Heckington — 82
Wrangle Pottery & Crafts, Wrangle, Boston — 74

GARDEN CENTRES
Baytree Nurseries, Weston, Spalding — 80
Dingle Nursery, Pilsgate — 78

PLACES TO VISIT & THINGS TO DO
Animal Gardens, Mablethorpe — 20
Ayscoughfee Hall Museum, Spalding — 8
Belvoir Castle, Grantham — 72
Brandy Wharf Cider Centre, Waddingham, Gainsborough
The Coachhouse, Wainfleet, Skegness — 76
Doddington Hall, Lincoln — 72
Elsham Hall Country Park, Brigg — 44
Fantasy World, Cleethorpes — 7
Fulbeck Hall, Grantham — 72
Funcoast World, Skegness — 7
Grimsthorpe Castle, Grimsthorpe, Bourne — 70
Guildhall Museum, Boston — 68
Heckington Windmill, Heckington — 82
Hemswell Antiques, Gainsborough — 86
Historic Boston — 10
Jungle World & Mini-Beasts Zoo, Cleethorpes — 18
Lincolnshire's Aviation Heritage. Coningsby — 32
Lincolnshire Aviation Heritage Centre, East Kirkby — 30
Lincolnshire Lively Attractions — Inside Front Cover
Lincolnshire & South Humberside Trust for Nature Conservation, Alford — 18
Lock & Castle Line, Castle Gate, Newark — 44
National Fishing Heritage Centre, Grimsby — 66
Natureland, Skegness — 20
Newark Air Museum, Newark — 30
Newark & Sherwood District — 13
Newgates Gallery, Stamford — 76
Northcote Heavy Horse Centre, Great Steeping, Nr Spilsby — 20
Our Little Farm, Plungar, Nottingham — 18
Pinchbeck Engine Museum, Pinchbeck — 8
The Pilgrim Fathers' Story, Worksop — 10
P.S. Lincoln Castle, Alexandra Dock, Grimsby — 6
Rutland Cottage Museum, Whaplode St Catherines, Nr Spalding — 68
South Holland, 'Heart of the Fens' — 8
Stamford Antiques Centre, Stamford — 82
Stamford Steam Brewery Museum, Stamford — 66
Stamford Shakespeare Company, Stamford — 40
Vina Cook Museum, Cromwell, Newark — 68